<u>Touched by Grace</u> is to my mind, a thoroughly enchanting book — I mean that quite literally, because from the very first pages, when the author shares the remarkable story of her own life, I felt myself being drawn into a sacred precinct — in Rashani's own word, a temenos — alive with the spirit of grace-filled women. A lovely companion of a book . . .

—Carol Lee Flinders, author of <u>Enduring Grace: Living Portraits of Seven Women Mystics</u>

If you look at anyone's Facebook feed, you're bound to see posts floating by that feature an image that combines some kind of artwork with a quote. It's become a popular and pithy way of transmitting spiritually uplifting information in recent years. But Rashani Réa, visionary artist, has been doing it for decades. Her beautiful cards have long adorned my living spaces, placed on altars or pinned to boards, and have been a source of delight, inspiration and comfort over the years. This book contains many favorites and some new offerings. It's a great book for just picking up in a moment when you need a boost, or an idea, or some excellent company, and to be reminded of the divine feminine and how that archetype of human experience speaks through the wise women of this world.

—Lara Owen, author of <u>Her Blood Is Gold and Growing Your Inner Light</u>

I've been waiting for Rashani's new book for a long time. I didn't know it consciously, but I had long appreciated her collage cards with quotations by women. Now it is a great joy to finally have a book, spanning eighteen years of her life, featuring wise words of women, many of whom Rashani has known and loved! Also, in <u>Touched by Grace</u>, Rashani shares her personal journey and gives us hints of how she came to her own awakening. This book contains many blessings that will help both women and men in their own journeys toward wisdom. Thank you, Rashani.

—Dorothy May Emerson, Unitarian Universalist minister, co-creator <u>Becoming Women of Wisdom: Marking the Passage into the Crone Years</u>

The magnetic force of feminine power. The loving embrace of the wise mother. The call to action of the fierce protectress. And the soft seduction of the sensual women. All of these are lovingly shared in Rashani Réa's collection of women's words.

Words from artists and priestesses, mothers, nuns, activists, and everything in between. Holy words whispered in the darkness. Words exclaimed from microphones. Words sung to the Earth in sorrow and exultation. Words that inspire us to rise, to do, to be, to embrace and embody our own creative potential, just as Rashani allowed them to inspire her to craft this collection of beautiful, honoring collages.

Let these words, drawn with love and couched in images that speak to the subconscious, inspire you into the depths and heights of your own feminine wisdom and expression.

—Niema Lightseed, poet and healing artist, <u>Medicinal Poetry</u>

Rashani Réa is a wise woman who knows she is not separate from all of life. She has been committed for decades to allowing the unique expression of that connection, through words and images, to become part of her own teaching. In this book she offers us a collection of word pearls from different women who live their truth and power, and offer their gifts in service to life. Each page offers a gem of wisdom to contemplate, inspire, and live by. That she honors others is one of Rashani's many gifts as she reminds us to take inspiration and guidance everywhere and that co-creation and collaboration is what we need to all be engaged in. Her art is so beautifully married to the words that they too seem like they were born to live together on the page and in our hearts. Keep this book close, it will be a good friend.

—Judith Ansara
www.sacredunion.com

More than ever in the human history do we need to acknowledge the qualities of the Deep Feminine and the wisdom of The Divine Mother—inherent to all the great religions and spiritual paths, and passed on to us by activists, poets and writers. We need it, and Gaia, the planet Earth with all its creations, longs for it.

I have never met anyone who knows so deeply the many faces of this powerful energy—from the tender to the fierce—as Rashani Réa does. Nor anyone who can communicate it so beautifully as she does in her art and poetry.

In the book Touched by Grace: Through a Temenos of Women Rashani has collected poems and quotes from 53 women that have inspired her, from the living Tibetan Buddhist Pema Chödrön to the ancient Christian mystic, Hildegard von Bingen. She has also included two of her own poems, among them 'The Unbroken'. And all of this is tied together by Rashani's delicate yet powerful collages.

What more could you possibly want from a book?! Rashani gives us hope and she believes that the collective awakening continues to unfold here on planet Earth. She is a midwife for this birth.

–Marie Louise Lefèvre, Film director and Publisher, The Wisdom Books
–Lise Lense-Møller, Film producer and Publisher, The Wisdom Books

I have known Rashani's work for at least 25 years, when she co-created **We'Moon '89** with me on the theme of living women **Spirit Healers**, of whom she is one, featuring her photographs and adorned with her elegant calligraphy. Touched by Grace is a continuation of her life's work — a book full of the beauty and wonder of Spirit healers through time, visionaries that have inspired the blossoming women's spirituality movement of today, framed in the devotional artistry of Rashani Réa.

–Musawa, founder, crone editor, publisher of We'Moon: Gaia Rhythms for Womyn
www.wemoon.ws

Because Rashani has managed to find her own way home through these words and images and memories, my heart suddenly finds it has a place to land. And because she has truly in this book, beyond all her others, stopped "drinking by the water's edge," has "thrown herself in," has "become the water," I am suddenly and dramatically relieved of a vast soul thirst, a woman thirst I did not even know I had! This is not really a book at all — it is a sacred place, a sanctuary of wisdom and love one can enter. I'm sure I will meet you there.

–Myriam Dyak, poet and co-founder, The Voice Dialogue Institute, Seattle

Rashani has been a way-shower for women for the past several decades while, humbly I know, she would say she was simply finding her own way. She continually creates from a place that for many of us is in need of the spark of illumination she provides through her creations. This book is a visual feast & testament, a scripture, a poetic gnostic bible of women's experience. She gives words life by weaving this very palpable life force of women's words and experience together, calling others to allow themselves the depth and richness of spectral experience that we all feel, but often isolate ourselves behind. Touched by Grace: Through a Temenos of Women beckons us forth to acknowledge and consciously become part of the sacred circle of women's experience in the world, and hold dear the value of this holy reality.

–Kayt Pearl, musician & performance artist

SACRED SPIRAL PRESS

P.O. Box 916, Na`alehu, Hawai`i
808 929-8043

ISBN-13: 978-0692670064
ISBN-10: 0692670068

Rashani is happy to share her creations and simply asks for a
donation towards a food forest, which she is planting at
her sanctuary, on the Big Island of Hawai`i.

Signed prints with these designs are also available.
Please contact her if you would like to
purchase or print any of the collages:

rashanirea@yahoo.com

Touched by Grace
Through a Temenos of Women

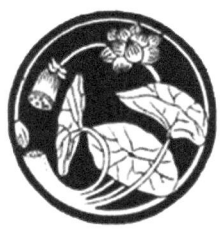

Words by Alice Walker, Anaïs Nin, Ann Herbert, Audre Lorde, Brooke Medicine Eagle, Buffie Johnson, Chellis Glendinning, Christina Harris, Clarissa Pinkola Estés, Dawna Markova, Deena Metzger, Dhyani Ywahoo, Dianthus, Dominie Cappadonna, Doreen Valiente, Dorothy Fadiman, Dorothy Hunt, Elizabeth Kübler-Ross, Emilie Conrad, Etty Hillesum, Gabrielle Herbertson, Geneen Roth, Helen Keller, Hildegard von Bingen, Holly Near, Jeanette Delmar, Jennifer Bonadio, Jett Psaris, Joanna Macy, Joan Halifax, Joan Larkin, Juju of Ka`u, Kate Wolf, Kathleen Raine, Kirtana, Kim Rosen, Lalla (also known as Lalleshwari), Ma Anandamayi, Marlena Lyons, Mirabai, Mother Teresa, Peace Pilgrim, Pema Chödrön, Rabia (also known as Rabi'a al-'Adawiyya al-Qaysiyya), Rashani Réa, Ricky Sherover-Marcuse, Sedonia Cahill, Sonia Johnson, Sappho, Starhawk, Susan Griffin, Toni Packer, and Tsultrim Allione.

Preface by Shayla Wright
Foreward by Britt Posmer

Other books by Rashani include:

Beyond Brokenness

My Bird Has Come Home: The Birthing of an Artist

A Cry of Windbells

Tao and the Moon

The Unfurling of an Artist: Early Collages and Calligraphy of Rashani Réa

Three Children's Stories

Welcome to the Feast: In Celebration of Wholeness

Is The Bowl Empty or Is It Filled with Moonlight?: Turning Words and Bodhi Leaves

The Way Moonlight Touches

Mahalo: Visual Koans for the Pathless Journey

Moonlight on a Night Moth's Wing: A Fusion of Image and Word

Shimmering Birthless: A Confluence of Verse and Image

An Unfolding of Love

True Golden Sand

Timeless Offerings

Always Choose Love

In addition, Rashani designed the cover and created a series of 35 collages
for the book Leaves from Moon Mountain by Dorothy Hunt.

With gratitude and love to the many women whose words are included in these pages,
to the Unknowable Muse, and to my mother—who allowed me to stay home
from school and create books when I was eight and nine years old.

Keeper of the Mysteries,
You have been here long before the spoken word.
In Your heart-mind stirred a vision of creation.
Long, so long ago
before the stars were constellations in the sky,
before the stars were scattered spirals of Your dance.
You lured the light from a sepalled dream,
while visions flowered in Your swelling womb.
Oh, Divine Mother,
birthing endless galaxies!
Your body is our universe.

From the silence
came Your whispered sound
followed by a heaving sigh,
then a molten song
of fire, water, earth and air.
Each element aware of being a Goddess child.
Creatrix of all beings,
we sing our praises to Your sacred name.

–Rashani Réa, 1988
(From the album, "Keeper of the Mysteries")

Mother of the universe
Who sustains all the world
Who is divine energy
Who removes all fears
Who gives liberation
Goddess of the waters
Residing in the lotus
Who is worshipped by God
Filled with wisdom
Who gives birth to all
Consort of victory
Who is within all beings
Maker of destiny
Mother of fire

Goddess of this planet
Who is energy everlasting
Who breathes as the children
Whose nature is joyful
Who accepts all surrender
The embodiment of mercy
Giver of ecstasy
Goddess of all goddesses
Who graces the universe
Giving divine protection
Beyond all beings
Goddess of the Earth
Breath of the wind
and The source of all that is.

–28 names of the Goddess, from a Hindu list of 108 names

In her notes to the reader on the origin of the collection, Rashani poses a question dear to my heart, and one which I believe is crucial to the radical reorientation of the contemporary Western psyche. She asks, what if "we knew from a young age that at the core of our being lies an inherent basic goodness/wholesomeness"?

The words and images that follow are the courageous and compassionate adornments of a lived responsiveness to such a view.

Though it is popular language to say we need to bring back the Feminine, I would point to the overwhelming evidence that She has always been here, carrying on the day-to-day operations of that threshold where the miraculous pours itself into the stream of the ordinary. Our estrangement is never total. Intimacy is Her natural province, and through Her we know ourselves inseparably at home.

The voices arising from the collective field of Woman assembled in these pages are unanimously affirming, direct, generous, and attentive. They dance with a wild and unstoppable creativity polished and illuminated by Rashani's detailed collages — delicate, mysterious, flowing, engendering the awareness that mixes body and spirit in the singleness of Love. Having first encountered Rashani through her selfless encouragement and advocacy of my own voice as an emerging poet and writer, I can attest to her unparalleled passion and vitality in service to her art. She is a crafter of worlds, both boundless and wise in the exercise of meticulous discrimination.

This book is a handful of jewels, each page an invitation to enlarge our recognition of the sacred. As a woman and artist, I find myself wanting to weave a stolen phrase here and there into a second skin that is both talisman and blessing. Tucking a feather behind my ear, I pray with Audre Lorde to, "...protect me from throwing any part of myself away."

We know little about the Feminine; She remains largely unmapped. For those of us that love Her, fiercely and from a need we scarcely understand, this is a great freedom. For if She is immeasurable and undiscovered possibility, then so are we. Our wholeness thrives not on definition but participation, and this is Her continuous gesture: to suffuse our consciousness with the vision of a reality made manifest through interconnected filaments of tenderness.

Recently, I felt the touch of Her lips upon my ear, wind before breath, in the opening lines of a poem. With gentle surety She whispered, "be unafraid/ of the movement of love/ it is only yourself/ dancing". Or in the words of the luminous Alice Walker, strung together in a hymn encircling the globe in the unity of Her benevolent enfolding,

"We have a beautiful mother
Her green lap immense
Her brown embrace eternal
Her blue body everything we know."

Preface by Shayla Wright

Through my friendship with Rashani, I know that her passion for the art and practice of collage is tireless. She lives in a flow of energy that carries her into creation in great waves of eros and inspiration. The speed at which she creates these complex and enthralling images amazes me. It speaks to a deep, instinctive, intuitive, self-emptying energy that guides her as she creates; a way of being that doesn't need to stop and think. From my perspective, this is a profoundly feminine way of being, which means that Rashani embodies in her creative process the essence of these poems, these words of wisdom and love.

The nature of my friendship with Rashani is precious to me: she is someone I have studied, practiced, laughed, and cried with. We have meditated together, contemplated the nature of reality, engaged in penetrating inquiry. I am grateful for this, as it has allowed me to see deeply into her nature. I know her as a lover of truth and also as a fierce devotee of our divine feminine nature. So this book feels to me like a natural expression of Rashani's heart: her longing to protect and nurture the intelligence and beauty of the sacred feminine.

You, dear reader, can move through this book in any way that you like. It doesn't ask you to begin at the beginning and proceed methodically towards the end. The wild freedom of the feminine permeates every part of it. I experience each page as a hologram, a world unto itself. On one level, the hologram is made of image, of meaning, of color; on a deeper level, it's composed of where the words and images come from— and where they carry us to—which will be utterly unique and mysterious for each one of us.

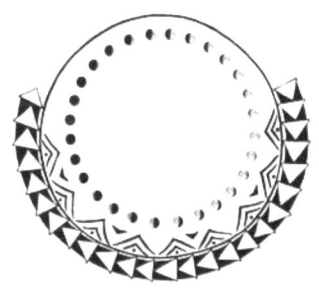

To say that I read this book does not really convey the truth of my experience. The beauty and depth of this book took my breath away when I first opened it. There is so much more than information and images here. Each page is an invitation and also a transmission. Some of you who open, read, drink in, and experience it may contact deep feelings that have been hiding inside you. Some of you may find burning questions emerging. Some of you may find nourishment for the soul, for the heart, or for the body. And some of you, like myself, may experience an inner prayer speaking to you from the page, asking you to stay here, for awhile, and drink deeply of what is being offered.

This happened to me near the end of the book, with the collage with words by Audre Lorde. The impact of the words dancing with this particular image claimed something in me, awakened a deep longing and knowing. My prayer for everyone who receives this living work of art is that we find the time and the receptivity to allow the full depth and power of it into our hearts, minds and bodies. May we allow ourselves to be touched and changed by what Rashani has created.

Introduction

"A temenos is a sanctuary, holy grove or holy precinct; a piece of land marked off from from common uses and dedicated to a goddess or god. The concept of temenos arose in classical Mediterranean cultures as an area reserved for worship of the sacred deities. In religious discourse in English, temenos has also come to refer to a territory, plane, receptacle or field of a deity or divinity.

C. G. Jung relates the temenos to the spellbinding or magic circle, which acts as a 'square space' or 'safe spot' where transformation can take place. This temenos resembles among others a symmetrical rose garden with a fountain in the middle (the 'squared circle') in which an encounter with the unconscious can be had and where these unconscious contents can safely be brought into the light of consciousness."

–https://en.wikipedia.org/wiki/Temenos

Dear reader,

We awaken together, interdependently, not in a vacuum. I am using the word "temenos" poetically here—referring to the women in this book as a morphogenic field. It was through, with and in this field of feminine compassion, wisdom, wonder, tenderness, fierce grace, non sentimental love, directness, and beauty that I discovered the 17-petalled lotus blooming in the center of my being.

I have been deeply influenced by the feminine principle, the Goddess, and by ancestral and contemporary women, from the time I was young. As a child I was enchanted with nature and intrigued by activism and art … and by the beauty, mystery and magnificence of the "Deep Feminine."

It is a joy to be creating this book, in celebration of the Eternal Feminine—as a way to pay homage to many of the women, some living and others deceased, who have accompanied me, physically and non physically, during this earth-walk.

For "bedtime stories," my father read to us from Simone de Beauvoir and Colette—two of his favorite writers—interspersed occasionally with Grimms' fairy tales. My mother read us haiku and tanka poetry and introduced us to Emily Dickinson, Edna Saint Vincent Millay, Gabriella Mistral and other women poets. And, as a lover of modern dance, she shared stories with us about Isadora Duncan—the feminist, revolutionary/pioneer of dance, and introduced us to Martha Graham, whom my father had danced with and created a series of lithographs of.

My childhood, in northern California, was an ongoing immersion into endless expressions of beauty; into the great unknowable Mystery. For this I remain tremendously grateful.

My childhood nickname, Tori, means "little bird" in Japanese. At the age of eight I was gifted with a small carved wooden stamp with my name on it. A Japanese friend of my parents had it made in Japan and presented it to me after seeing a series of sumi-e brush paintings, which I had created as illustrations for a book of my haiku poetry.

When I was nine years old, my parents took my brothers and me to Telegraph Hill, in San Francisco, to see my father's murals in Coit Tower. "The Coit Tower murals were painted during a particularly disruptive period in U.S. History. Depression related economic challenges led to much discussion about alternate forms of government. A four day general strike (Bloody Thursday) accompanied by widespread rioting in San Francisco triggered an eighty-three day West Coast Waterfront Strike in 1934. Coit Tower muralists protested and picketed at the tower when Diego Rivera's mural commissioned for Rockefeller Center in New York City was destroyed.

The youngest of the muralists, George Albert Harris," (my father) "painted a mural called 'Banking and Law.' In the mural, the world of finance is represented by the Federal Reserve Bank and a stock market ticker (in which stocks are shown as declining) and law is illustrated by a law library. Some of the book titles that appear in the law library, such as 'Civil, Penal, and Moral Codes', are legitimate, while others list fellow muralists as authors, in a joking manner."

–https://en.wikipedia.org/wiki/Coit_Tower

Art and activism were in my blood!

Three years later, in 1964, following the death of my 19-year-old brother, my family traveled through Europe for nearly a year. My father took a sabbatical while writing a book on European art history and wanted to share with us some of his favorite places.

Our journey began in England, at Stonehenge, on the Summer Solstice, witnessing a Druid ceremony at dawn. I still remember that long ago morning, watching the sun rise through the ancient Heel Stone and standing speechless while a group of Druids entered the circle and performed their annual ceremony—as they and their predecessors had done for hundreds and hundreds of years. We were there with friends, amidst a small group of fascinated onlookers, humbled by the ancestral presence of the stones and honored to be in the presence of the Druids, who welcomed us with loving kindness.

My family also visited the nearby megalithic site in Avebury that day and for the following twelve months we visited many other Megalithic and Neolithic sites, as well as numerous museums, monasteries, temples, ruins, prehistoric caves, shrines, abbeys, churches, cloisters, and magnificent cathedrals. Many of the places we visited were ancient goddess-worshipping sites. Years later, it occurred to me that the year in Europe with my family was an initiation of sorts into the ancient Goddess Mysteries.

In the oldest myths, the creative essence of the universe was always female. The ancient, pre-Christian mythology of most of Europe was deeply woman-centered.

After four and a half months of traveling—in Great Britain, Sweden, Denmark, Germany, Holland, Austria, and what was then Yugoslavia—we decided to spend the winter in Greece.

My early impressions of Greece were magical and remain imprinted in my memory: The openness and joy of the Greek people and how they taught us to dance… Wandering through the palaces and citadels in Mycenae, where my brother found a small head of an ancient terra-cotta figurine—which we took to the archaeological museum… The timelessness of the Cycladic female figurines, which many archaeologists believe are representations of the Goddess, and/or companions to Her… Learning about Plato and Socrates and the difference between mythos and logos.

"Plato described the two different ways of approaching truth as mythos and logos. Mythos is a more silent, intuitive way of looking at reality and logos is more of a scientific, discursive, logical way, and we need both. We've always needed logistic thought, if only to sharpen an arrow correctly.

We've always been aware that there are two ways of approaching truth, one through reason and science and the other through an intuitive knowing. The word mythos comes from the Greek word which means to close the mouth or close the eyes. Mystery and mysticism come from the same root. So they are associated with a sense of darkness, with going into a realm where you don't see very clearly, where things are more obscure and will remain obscure. It is also a realm of silence rather than wordy thought. We approach this kind of knowing in art. At the end of a great symphony or when you've listened to a great poem there's often nothing to say. You're being pushed beyond rational thoughts and distinctions into a silent intuitive space."

–Excerpt from an interview with Karen Armstrong, author of The Great Transformation and The History of God

The majority of the figurines found at Mycenae were female and the largest complete wall painting in Mycenae was of three female figures, most likely priestesses or goddesses. After spending a day in Mycenae and several days in Delphi and Athens, we took a ferry to the island of Crete, where we stayed for three months. We rented a house surrounded on three sides by a vineyard—across the road from Knossos, the ancient Minoan goddess-worshipping center.

Our "winter nest" was a ten-minute walk from the oldest known city in Europe. Our home became a harbor for several international travelers we had met during our journey. I celebrated my 13th birthday at the Palace of Knossos and was enamored with the Minoan pottery and frescoes, and particularly by the Snake Goddesses, most of which are now in the Heraklion museum.

The palace of Knossos was the ceremonial and political center of the Minoan civilization and culture; the perfect place to turn thirteen! Due to the prevalence of female images, it is believed that the Minoans worshiped primarily goddesses, which has been described as a "matriarchal religion."

Everywhere we went, there were legends about ancient goddesses and gods. This pantheon of deities was amazing. I was fascinated to discover that the Greek oracles were always women and that snakes were associated with the oracles, such as Pythia, the Oracle of Delphi. We were told that they were mediums for the Earth Goddess, Gaia, before they became the servants of Apollo.

As winter began turning into spring, we visited several of the Aegean islands and made our way slowly through Italy, France, Spain and Portugal. I enjoyed wandering through the temples in Paestum and Pompeii and discovering the Roman goddesses, most of whom had Greek counterparts.

I felt very at home in Florence, where we spent a month with my father's good friend, Raimondo Puccinelli. Raimondo and Esther, his wife, shared with us their favorite museums, parks, theaters, and monuments. I still remember the day that Esther Puccinelli told us about the miraculous Black Madonnas, which she had been researching for many years.

"The Black Madonnas are often the central image of honor in the cathedrals, caves, and mountain top shrines and sanctuaries where they are found, and are very often considered miraculous… The miraculous is found in abundance in Italy. Testimonials come from the people themselves over the centuries through offerings, and from written accounts of legendary or authenticated miracles.

Umberto Cordier has published an Italian-language guide to 600 such miraculous sites in Italy, recounting a brief summary of the church or sanctuary's central miracle. Although miracle stories of saints and other entities are included, Mary is the dominant miracle-worker…

My investigations along with the research of numerous scholars show a long history of honoring female divinity on the Italian peninsula that predates Jesus and perhaps any male deity. In addition to Greek and Roman goddesses, there were Asian, African and indigenous goddesses that were venerated. Archeological finds of figurines, painted pots and vases from Neolithic (New Stone Age) settlements and caves across the

Italian peninsula indicate the presence of the sacred feminine; carved female figures reach back into the Paleolithic, or Old Stone Age, for their origin.

Lucia Chiavola Birnbaum, a feminist cultural historian who has written extensively about Black Madonnas, traces the ultimate origin of all dark mother images to Africa. She cites genetic, cultural and archeological evidence, to show that Italy lies along paths of African migrations 50,000 years ago to all continents of the earth. Such a long recognition of a divine female is not easily cast aside. Historical records show that pre-Christian goddesses were invoked for healing and protection, and were associated with miracles. As the Catholic Church became the dominant religion over the centuries in Italy, replacing the existing spiritual practices, Mary, as the only prominent female, was the natural heir."

–Excerpt from Blood Relics: Menstrual Roots of Miraculous Black Madonnas in Italy by Mary Beth Moser, Ph.D

I discovered that throughout Europe, especially in France, there are more than 500 Black Madonnas, painted and carved in wood or stone. They are found mostly in the Catholic churches and crypts, and a few can be found in museums. My most favorite was the Black Madonna in Rocamadour, France, which possibly dates back to the 9th century. (I visited her many times, during the eighteen years that I lived down the road from Rocamadour.)

"For several centuries, politically dominant Christians destroyed the temples and shrines of the pagan goddesses in the name of their male divinity. Christian churches and cathedrals were developed at these holy sites and named for Mary, who had been previously designated Mother of God by the early church fathers. As such, she absorbed most of the attributes of the great goddesses, including the titles, Seat of Wisdom and Queen of Heaven. As Athena before her, she was and is still the powerful and comforting mediatrix between her devotees and a male godhead. Nonetheless, for two thousand years, by the god-given authority of the Church, she could not be called "goddess" and still remains officially subordinate to her son, Jesus."

–Excerpt from Who Said, "God Said"? The Truth behind the Myth of Female Inferiority by Carol Wolf Winters, Ph.D.

Throughout high school I designed many collages and studied calligraphy with Sister Monica Julie, a student of Sister Corita, later known as Corita Kent. Corita was a passionate peace activist, a prolific artist, an embodiment of Quan Yin—the Goddess of Mercy and Compassion—and one of my earliest mentors.

Art and activism were my two great loves and were like two wings of a glorious bird. My being took flight—uplifted by the inspiration of artists and musicians, particularly those who used their creations in behalf of social justice. Activism was a spiritual practice and seemed like a natural unfolding of social awareness.

My first collages with words were created when I was fourteen years old. Within days of this "catching fire" I began cutting and tearing origami paper and writing poems across layers of color, mesmerized by the subtle textures and how translucent some papers were and how others appeared opaque.

From the age of fourteen to seventeen, I hand-lettered several books; most of which were filled with colorful collages. As a junior in high school I spent several months creating a book of collages, with quotes by artists, for an English Class assignment. It was later published as The Unfurling of an Artist.

In June of 1970, a few months after the book was finished, my family moved to Europe. I continued interweaving art and activism and the unstoppable creativity which poured through me morphed from collages into singing and teaching; later into pottery and eventually into the joyous art of motherhood. Throughout the 1970's, I was involved in the feminist movement in France, England and Denmark and my life was impacted by several prominent feminist theologians, activists, poets, and writers. I revisited many of the ancient goddess-worshipping sites throughout Europe, which I had visited with my family when I was 12 and 13 years old—and discovered many more.

In 1975 I traveled with my son to New York, to visit my closest childhood friend, Dwarka, who had recently returned from several years in India. He had been one of the cooks in the Kainchi Dham ashram of Neem Karoli Baba—known also as "Maharajji"—and I hadn't seen him for several years, since he visited my family, in Engand, on his way to India.

After Maharajji's death, in 1973, Dwarka returned to the United States with several other devotees of Maharajji. The day before I returned to France, Dwarka handed me a large pile of photographs and asked me to choose whichever ones I would like to take with me. (In the Hindu tradition it is customary to have photographs of saints and teachers in one's home.)

I spent several hours looking carefully at the photographs; looking into the eyes of many female and male sadhus, gurus, and saints—knowing very little about them, yet experiencing their essence by the light emanating from their eyes. The photographs that called to me were two pictures of Ma Anadamayi, who instantly became a beloved presence in my life.

Her gaze was both a window, through which I glimpsed eternity—and a mirror, in which I saw habitual aspects of my identity effortlessly dissolve. It was several years later that I discovered that Ma was described as "the most perfect flower the Indian soil has produced."

Ma Anandamayi refused to be called a guru. She maintained that "all paths are my paths" and repeatedly said, "I have no particular path." She was a blissful rebel, who advocated spiritual equality for women and was one of the first teachers in India who declared that a guru was not necessary in order to attain Self realization.

She opened the sacred thread ritual to women, which was previously performed only by men, for centuries, and wandered through India for years—being lovingly adored and cared for wherever she went.

In August of 1982, three months after my mother's death, my son and I traveled to India, where we were hoping to spend time with Ma Anandamayi. Unfortunately, she left this earthly realm on August 27th, in Dehradun, north of New Delhi, shortly after we arrived in India.

Though I never met her in the flesh, she remains a loving presence in my life. I was overjoyed to discover that her only ashram outside of India is on the Big Island of Hawai`i, where I currently live.

During the 80's I was also inspired by ecofeminists, eco-philosophers and feminist psychologists.

"Ecofeminism describes movements and philosophies that link feminism with ecology. The term is believed to have been coined by the French writer Françoise d'Eaubonne in her book Le Féminisme ou la Mort (1974). From arguments that there are particular and significant connections between women and nature, ecofeminism interprets their repression and exploitation in terms of the repression and exploitation of the environment. Ecofeminists believe that these connections are illustrated through traditionally "feminine" values such as reciprocity, nurturing and cooperation, which are present both among women and in nature. Women and nature are also united through their shared history of oppression by a patriarchal Western society."

–https://en.wikipedia.org/wiki/Ecofeminism

In the mid 80's I attended a Heroine's Journey Conference. Several feminist writers, psychologists, and Jungian analysts were suggesting that The Hero's Journey is actually not appropriate for women's life journeys. They believed that the model of The Hero's Journey does not adequately address the psycho-spiritual journey of women.

From the hero's perspective, we have been taught to believe that we must (symbolically) enter a labyrinth and "slay a minotaur." Consequently, our psyche is already conditioned to expect combat and violence. As a result of this notion, women—and probably some men as well— are sometimes afraid of, or have an aversion to, the inner journey.

The speakers at the conference had done extensive research into pre-Christian goddess mythology and contemporary psychology. They were suggesting that the Heroine's Journey is different than the Hero's. Though I don't remember who it was, or her exact words, one of the keynote speakers—a Buddhist— asked a question, which radically changed my way of perceiving life!

Something to the effect of: "Who would we be if we had been taught at a young age that at the center of the labyrinth is a seventeen-petalled lotus flower, not a monster?"

In other words, if we knew from a young age that at the core of our being lies an inherent basic goodness/wholesomeness, our life journeys may be quite different. Contrary to the Christian notion of original sin, Buddhism understands that human beings are fundamentally good; that our most basic, intrinsic qualities are warmth, openness, and intelligence and that our essential nature is awake, clear and gentle.

….. I raised a son and spent eighteen years renovating a 17th century stone farmhouse in the south of France. My creativity expanded in many directions and designing collages was temporarily left behind.

In 1986 I recorded my first album; a collection of songs, poems, and chants to the Divine Feminine, which I had been gathering and writing for several years. Sarah Benson and Molly Scott, two gifted sound healers and musicians who I had met in Massachusetts, joined me for two weeks and we recorded—often long into the nights—in churches, caves, crypts, cloisters and cathedrals near my home.

I remember vividly our morning recording in the crypt at Rocamadour. The presence of the Black Madonna was powerful. Her essence permeated the entire crypt. We arrived at 5 a.m.—before the onslaught of tourists arrived. We had spent the entire previous night recording in a beautiful little church in the village of Orniac, which was a few kilometers from my home.

While driving from Orniac to Rocamadour, a large barn owl flew into the windshield of our small van and we found her motionless on the road. I held her limp body in my hands while five of us stood in a small circle, stunned, beneath a thin crescent moon. We spontaneously toned for her, in harmony, for several minutes. Suddenly, she lifted her head, looked into our eyes as if to thank and bless each of us, and opened her magnificent wings! As tears of amazement poured down our cheeks, this winged miracle disappeared into the darkness. We felt as if we had been blessed by "the owl of Athena." Athena (Minerva in Roman mythology) was the Virgin Goddess of wisdom and insight.

Our final recording was in Saint-Étienne Cathedral, in the town of Cahors. Every Saturday, for many years, after shopping in the Cahors market, I would enter this majestic, double-domed cathedral and offer songs to the Goddess. Some time in the early 1980's I received a silent invitation to "bring the Goddess back" by recording an album of songs and chants in Her honor.

I graciously accepted the invitation.

The acoustics of Saint Étienne cathedral are similar to the Taj Mahal. Sarah accompanied Molly and me on her silver flute and we filled the cathedral with soetry (songs and poetry) until the sun rose the following morning…..

Merlin Stone, author of When God Was a Woman, wrote a wonderful endorsement for the cassette and sent a copy to her friend, Buffie Johnson. Buffie had spent more than forty years researching artifacts, statues, and the art of the Goddess from the Middle East, Europe, Asia, and Africa.

One day I received a call from Buffie, asking if she could visit my son and me in southern France. She had heard that we lived near the cave of Peche Merle, which she was writing about. She was ecstatic at the thought of being able to enter the cave, which she had researched for many years!

My son and I received Buffie with great joy and she shared with us the soon-to-be-published galley proofs of her extraordinary book, Lady of the Beasts: Ancient Images of the Goddess and Her Sacred Animals. It was published by Harper & Row the following year.

While staying with us she was doing final edits and it was an honor to take her to the cave of Peche Merle, which was less than twenty kilometers from our home. I also took Buffie to see some nearby Neolithic dolmens and sang for her in Saint Étienne cathedral—and in the small chapel, above the crypt, at Rocamadour, where the Black Madonna sits like Isis, holding her son.

The following year, when I was living with my son in northern California, I traveled to Oregon to visit some friends. In Portland, I discovered a wonderful art gallery, called "In Her Image." The owners of the gallery were planning a show and asked if I would like to submit anything.

I hadn't designed a collage in more than eighteen years. The topic, "Women's Erotic Art," was intriguing so I said I would consider the invitation. "Erotic" for me was both sexual and spiritual—since both engender timelessness, egolessness, and fathomlessness.

I returned to California, began re-reading several of my favorite poets, and designed a series of collages— incorporating the words of several women poets, including a few poems of my own. The creative fire of collaging, which had been birthed twenty-two years earlier, whose embers had lain fallow for many years, was suddenly re-ignited!

While attending the opening of the show I met the founder of the We'Moon calendar, who asked if I would like to design and hand-letter the next issue of the almanac.

"The We'Moon almanac is an empowering datebook and multicultural earth spirited calendar, which features art and writing by and about women: an exploration of women's experience and perspectives, a goddess-inspired creation from the growing edge of global women's culture. We'Moon datebooks include full daily lunar and astrological information in a week-at-a-glance format, a lunar month-at-a-glance section, and a comprehensive introduction to astrology, Sun / Moon / Earth cycles, and seasonal Holy Days. Art, prose and poetry by hundreds of gifted contributors from around the world are organized into 13 themed moon-chapters, variously exploring the current years' theme."

–http://wemoon.ws/wemoon.html

I interviewed and photographed twelve multicultural women, hand-lettered the entire almanac and included a short bio and photograph of myself for the 13th lunation. During the months that I was creating the We'Moon almanac, I continued designing collages—incorporating words of Hildegard von Bingen and several other women. Eternal feminine wisdom was a timeless healing balm—appearing as many voices of the One Great Mother.

A few years later, when my son went to join his father in Canada, I returned to the U.S. for awhile and lived with Buffie Johnson in her spacious studio/loft apartment, in Soho. Buffie was nearing eighty and needed assistance with day to day tasks, such as shopping, preparing food and cleaning. I was happy to be of service to such a remarkable woman. When her eyesight began to fail, she returned to abstract painting. Often she would be focused on her series of abstract canvases while I was designing collages in the small room above her studio.

"Buffie Johnson's last series of paintings had their roots back in that research trip to Europe in 1954 when she had befriended Carl Jung. She and Jung had many meetings and his insights into the origins and workings of human consciousness were to excite her own exploration of symbolism. Her Numbering Series are a sequence of abstract canvases where numbered forms are suspended in a vivid blue picture space."

–http://sugswritersblog.blogspot.com/2013/02/the-31-women-number-three-buffie-johnson.html

During the following twenty-seven years I created several hundred collages, many of which were printed as greeting cards and others, which have been published in my books. The collages you are about to see are from "The Women's Collection" and a few of them are from "The Amerindian Collection," which I created in 1991, in honor of Leonard Peltier. (Hence: you will see the names of certain tribes on a few of them.)

These particular collages are hand-lettered and were created between 1988 and 2005. (My more recent collages have been created with fonts.) Several of the women whose words you are about to read have been my mentors and teachers and more than half of them are beloved friends and acquaintances.

As I write this, I can hear Holly Near singing, "Oh, there's something about the women in my life!"

Indeed.

Having journeyed deeply during the past fifty years with numerous women, from many traditions, I am delighted to be sharing this book with you. Again and again, worldwide, women reflect the fundamental warmth, openness and intelligence, which is the essence of what we *are.*

Reflecting back over/through the past several decades of my life, I am amazed, inspired, and touched by the intricate and diverse tapestry of women who were—and continue to be—a wise, loving, tender, powerful, fierce, omnipresent, courageous, caring, daring, sustainable support system, sangha, and sacred web of love and life. Yes, a holy temenos!

Some are 'unsung sheroes' and others are widely recognized women. And ALL of them are inextricably interwoven into my life, as well as into the collective awakening, which continues to unfold here on planet Earth. These are some of the many women who have accompanied me on my pathless journey. My whole being overflows with boundless love and gratitude for each of these precious women.

In the words of Ma Anandamayi:

"One is, in their own Self, the wanderer, the exile, the home-coming and the home."

Jai Ma!

Rashani Réa,
Imbolc, 2016

Some Unsaid Things

I was not going to say
how you lay with me
        nor where your hands went
        & left their light impressions
                nor whose face was white
                as a splash of moonlight
                        nor who spilled the wine
                        nor whose blood stained the sheet

                nor which one of us wept
                to set the dark bed rocking
        nor what you took me for
        nor what I took you for
    nor how your fingertips
    in me were roots

light roots torn leaves put down—
nor what you tore from me
nor what confusion came
of our twin names
    nor will I say whose body
    opened, sucked, whispered
        like the ocean, unbalancing
        what had seemed a safe position

                        -Joan Larkin

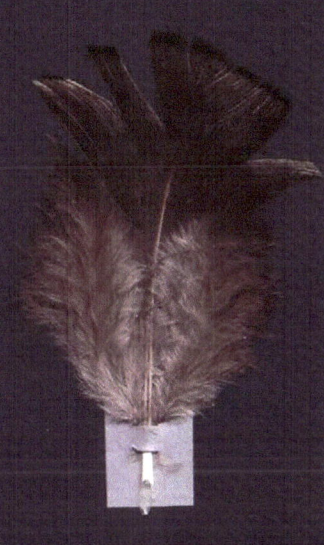

Rashani
25. 1. 88

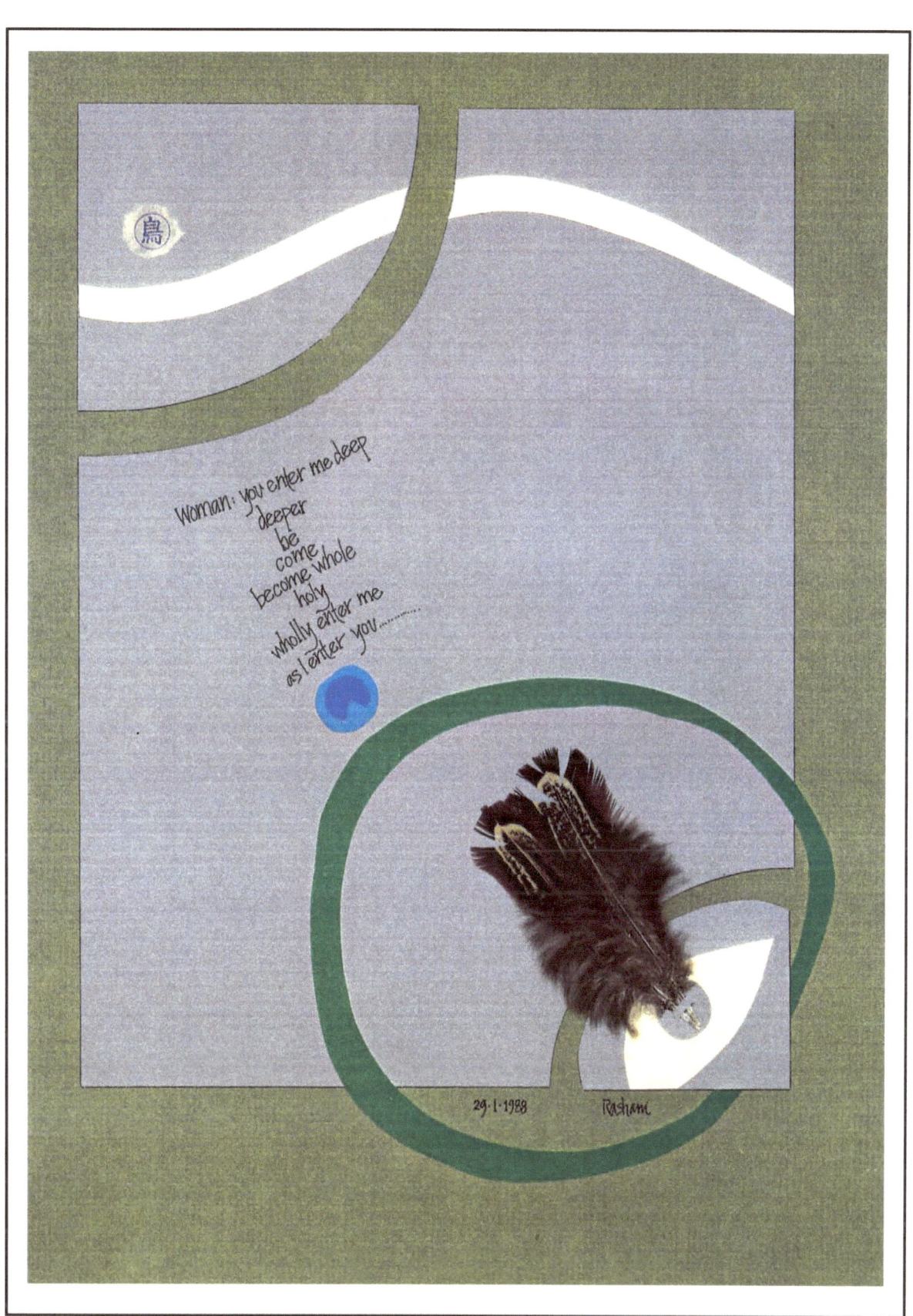

Woman: you enter me deep
deeper
be
come
become whole
holy
wholly enter me
as I enter you.......

29·1·1988   Rashani

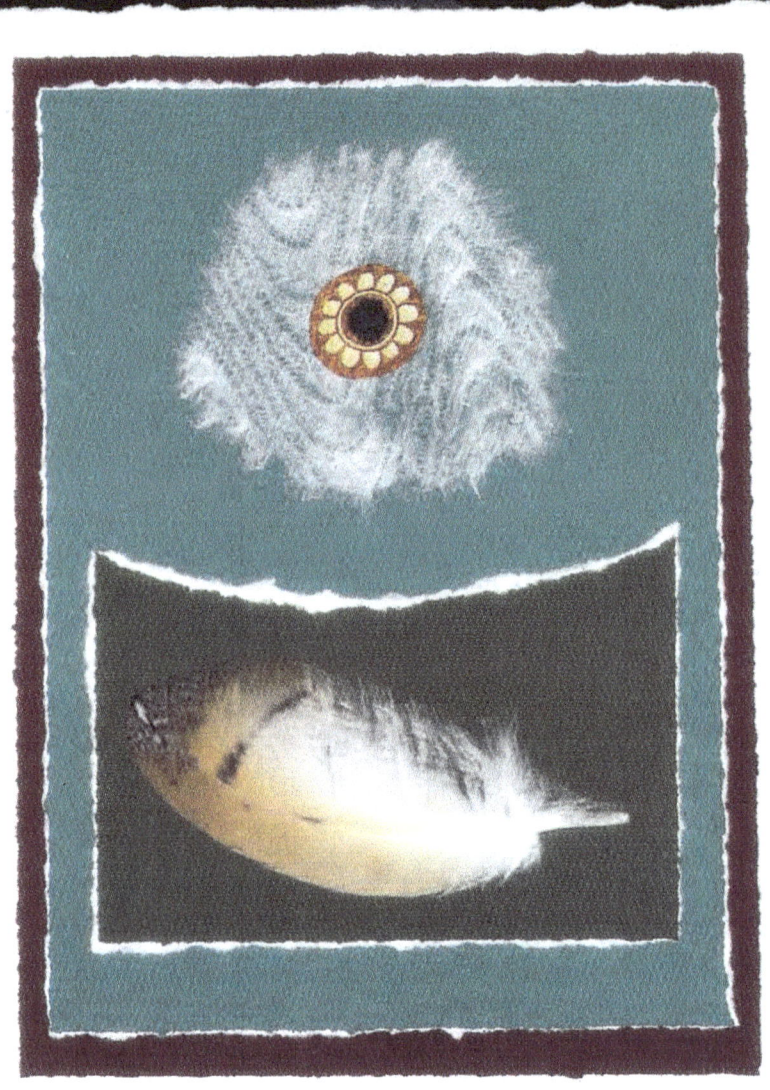

The experience gained in darkness sheds light on the whole being and through this experience we are irrevocably changed and empowered.

Tsultrim Allione

To sustain life as we know it, we all must act. We must all become "environmentalists." Our planet depends on it.......

Work together with one heart

Anonymous

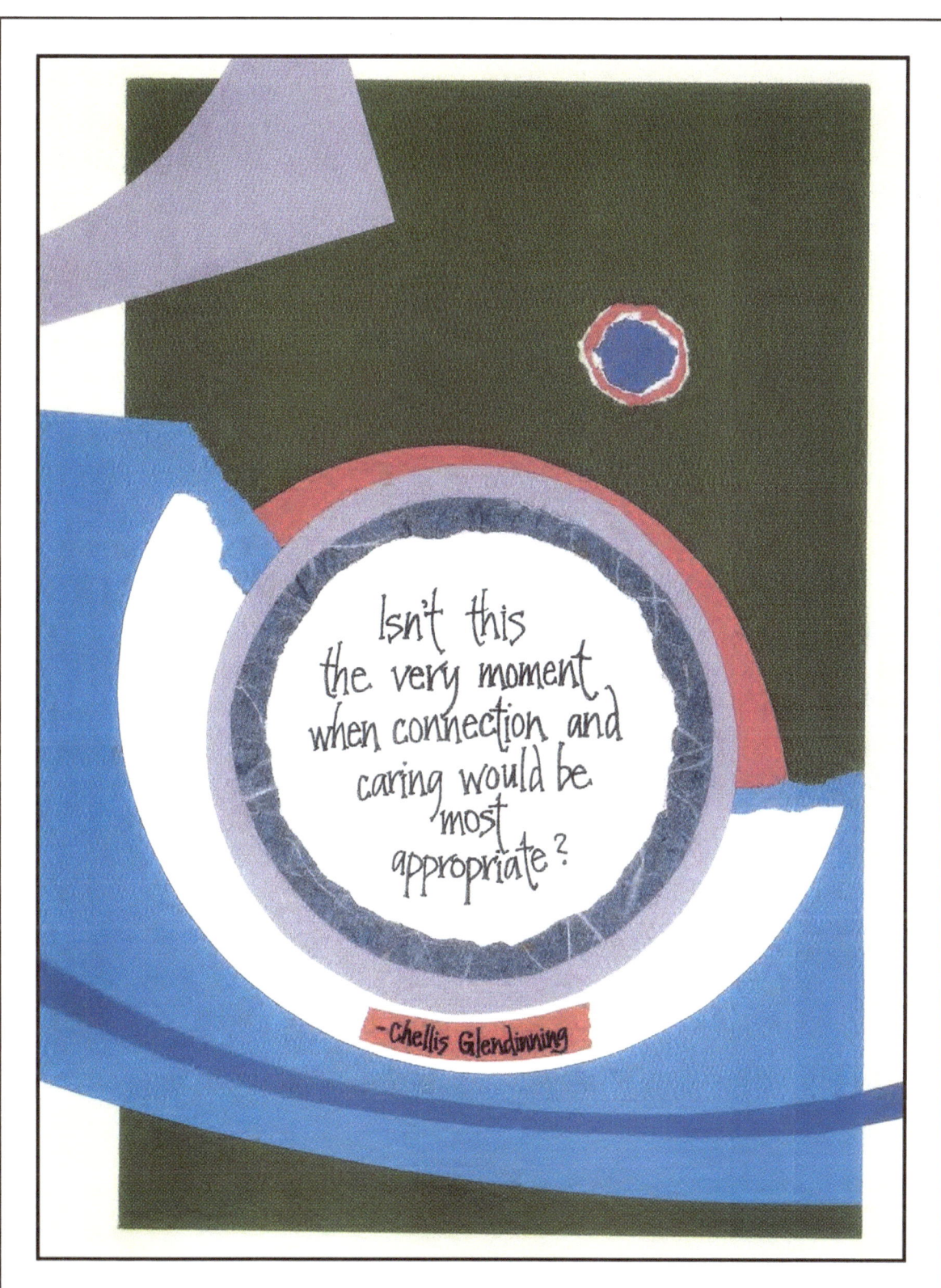

Isn't this
the very moment
when connection and
caring would be
most
appropriate?

—Chellis Glendinning

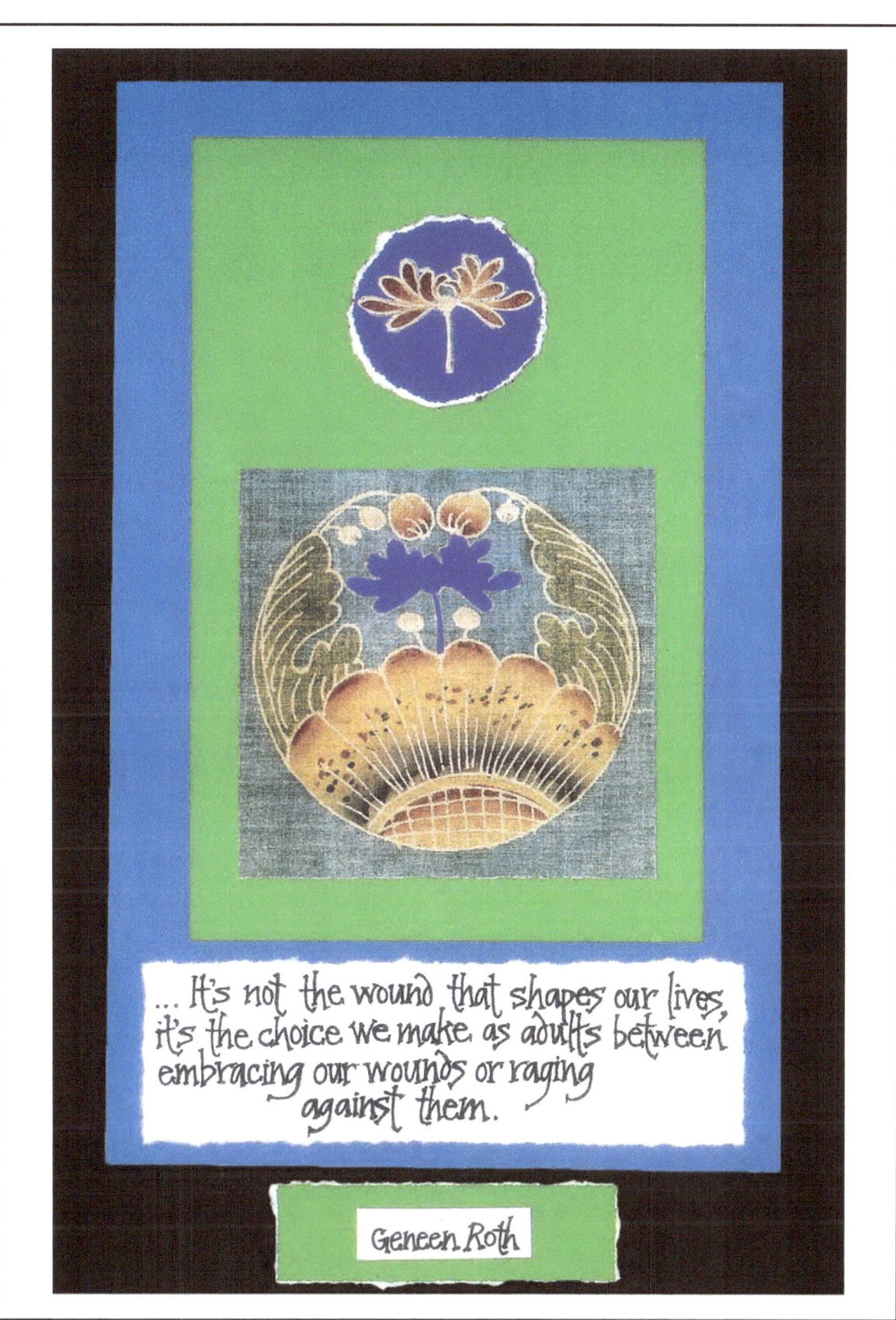

... It's not the wound that shapes our lives, it's the choice we make as adults between embracing our wounds or raging against them.

Geneen Roth

True forgiveness and love arise naturally,
effortlessly, from the silence of a heart
broken all the way open .

Gangaji

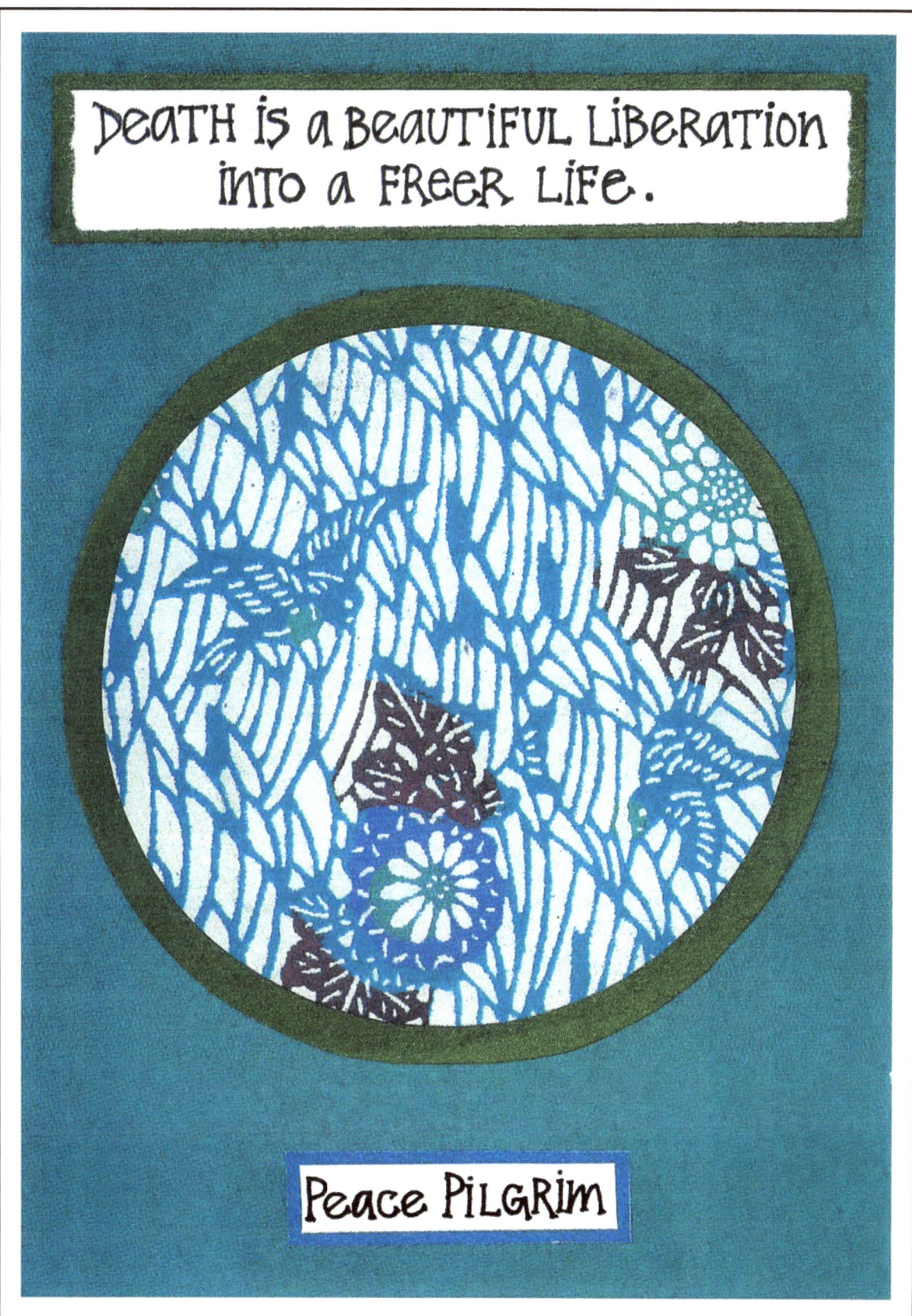

DEATH is a BEAUTIFUL LIBERATION into a FREER LiFE.

Peace PiLGRiM

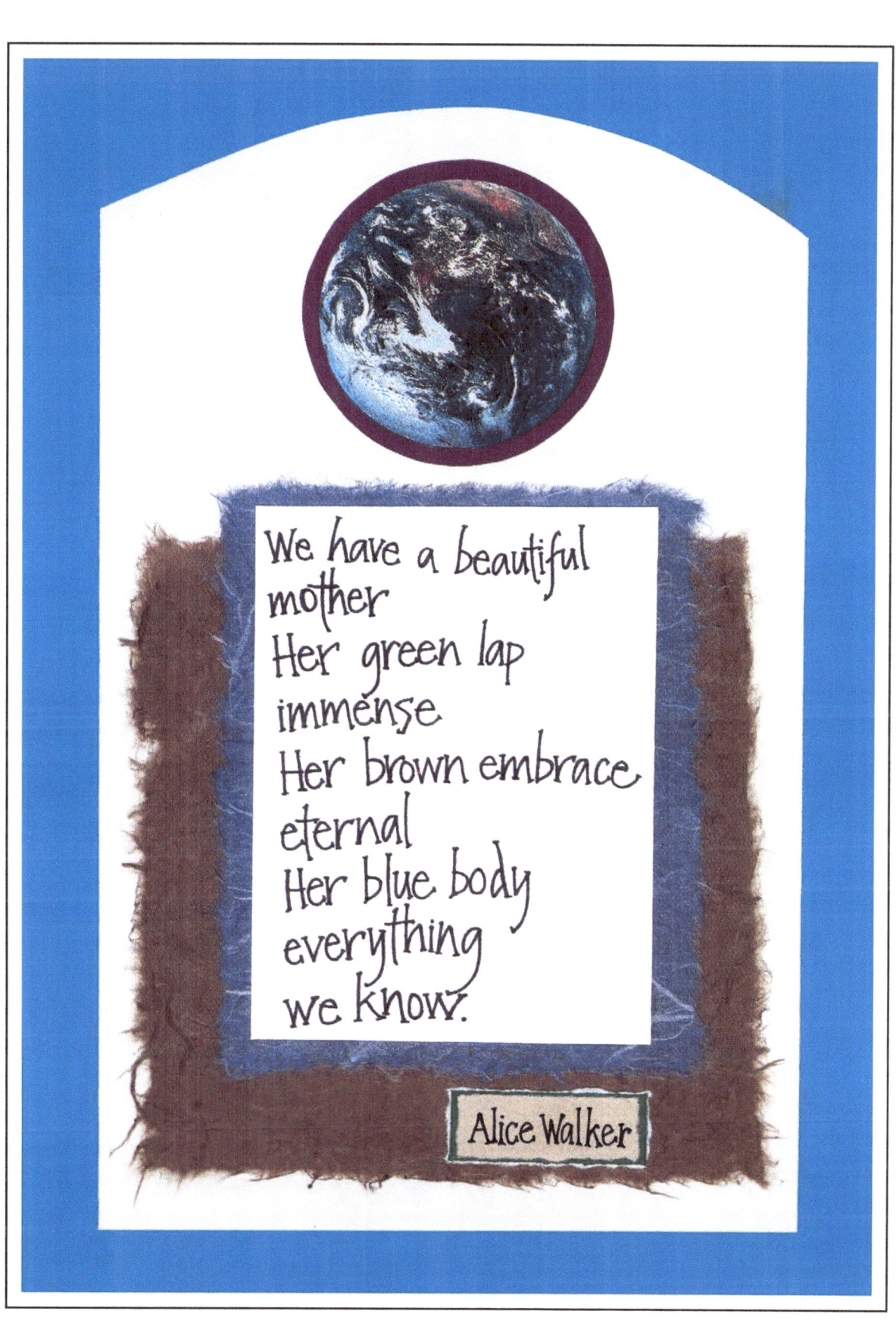

We have a beautiful
mother
Her green lap
immense.
Her brown embrace
eternal
Her blue body
everything
we know.

Alice Walker

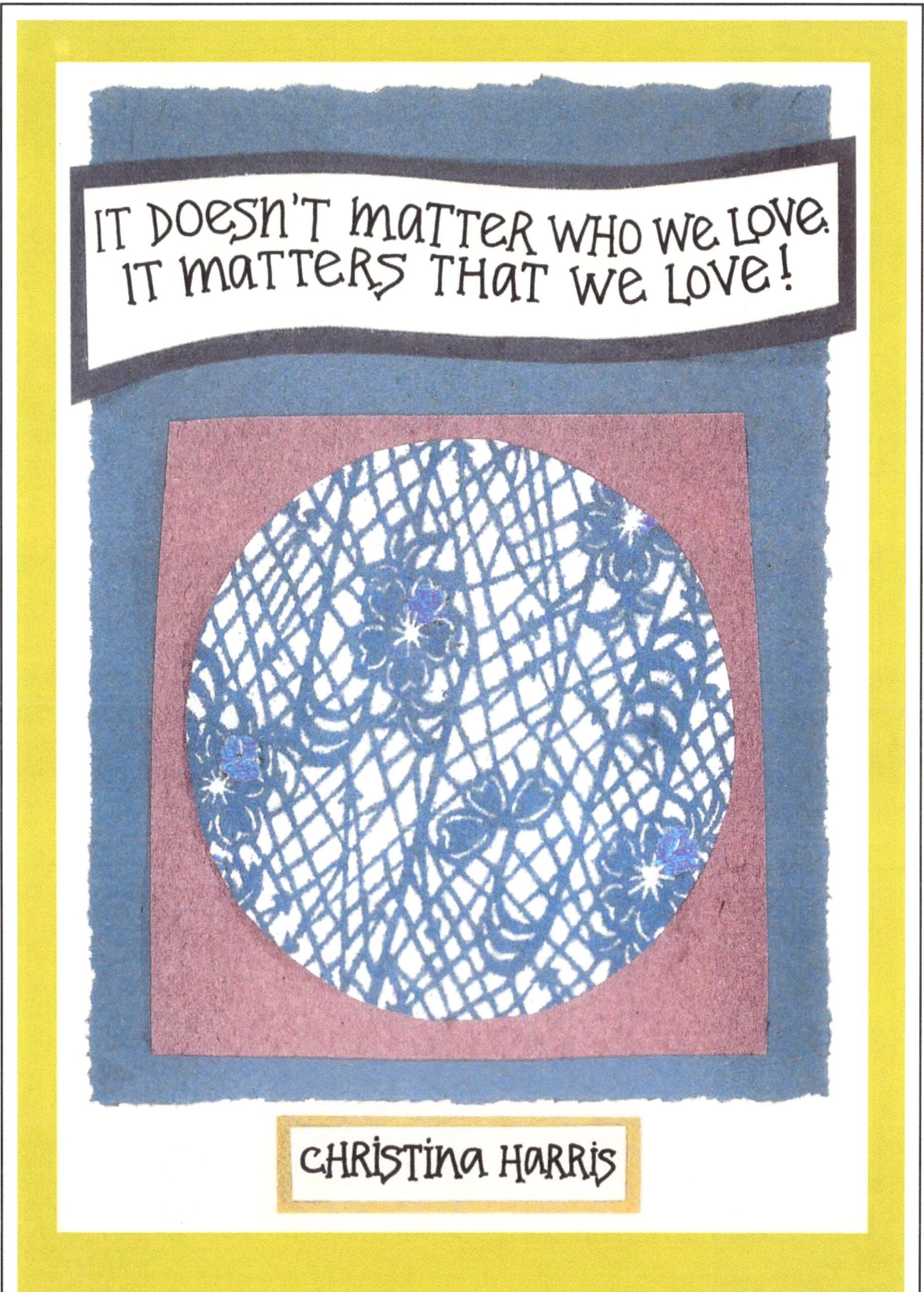

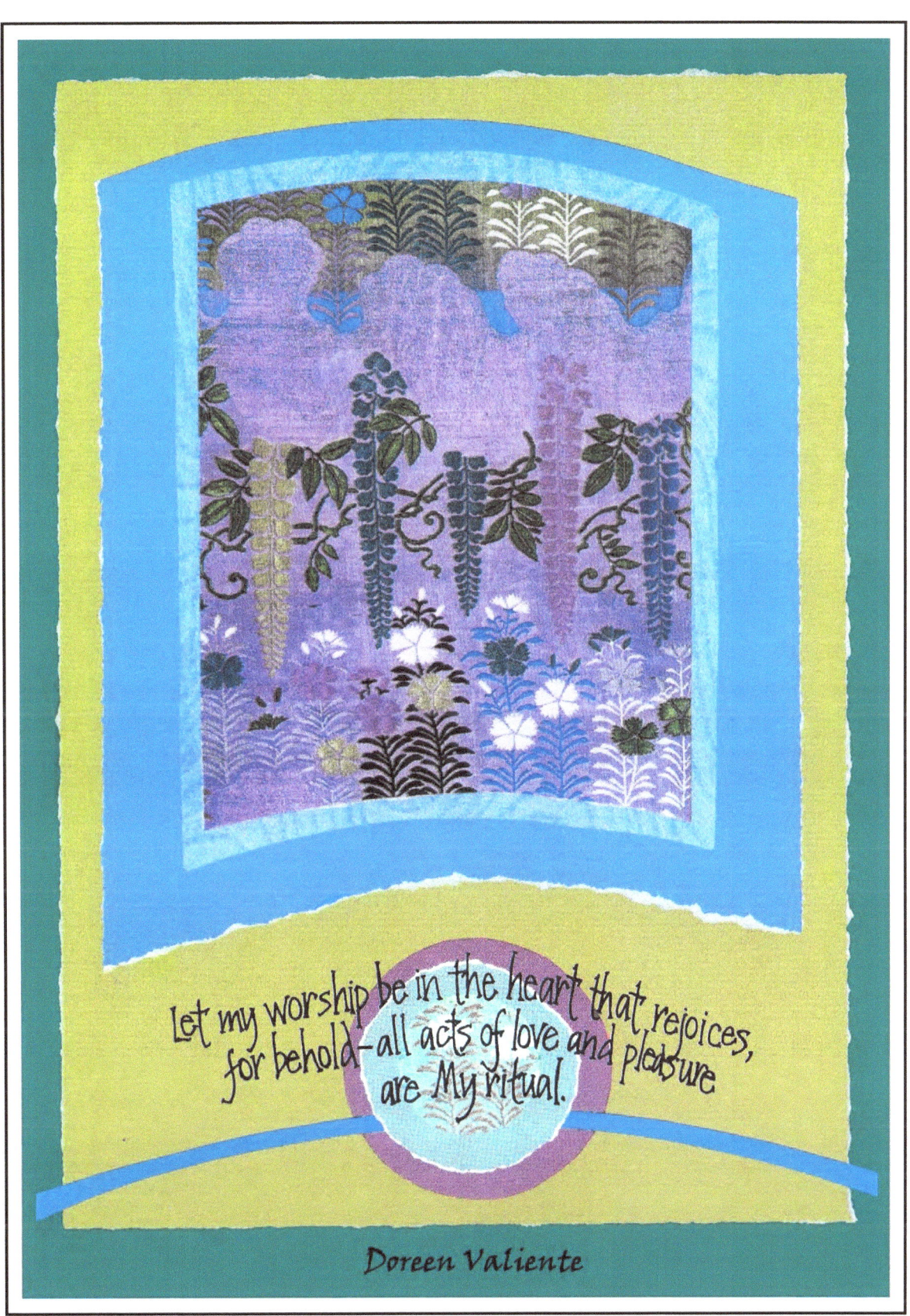

Let my worship be in the heart that rejoices, for behold—all acts of love and pleasure are My ritual.

Doreen Valiente

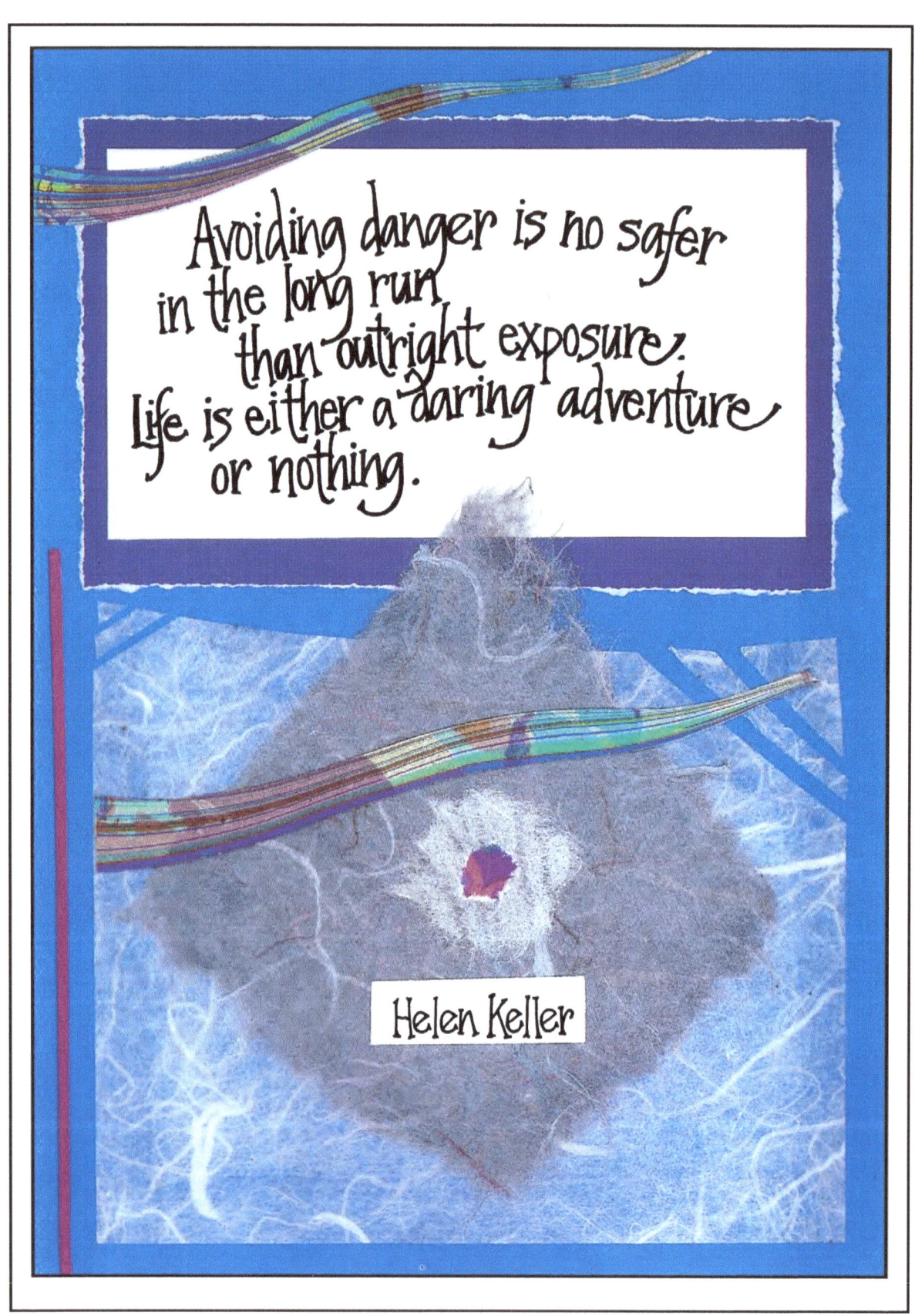

Avoiding danger is no safer in the long run than outright exposure. Life is either a daring adventure or nothing.

Helen Keller

Death is a bridge whereby the lover rejoins the Beloved.

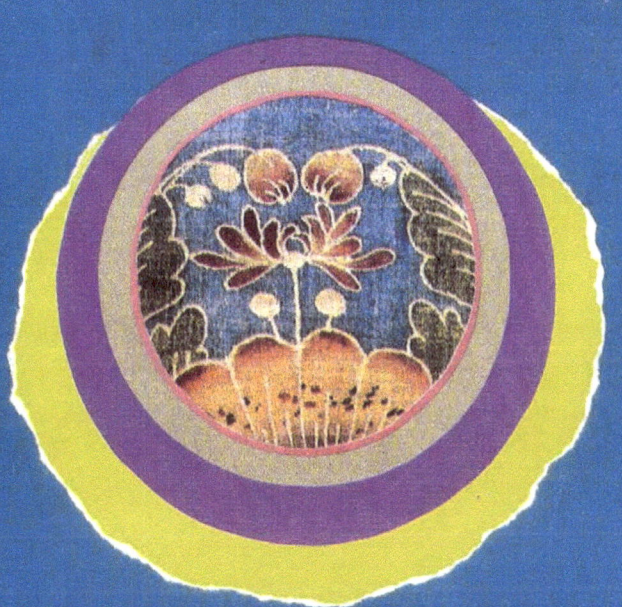

Rabia

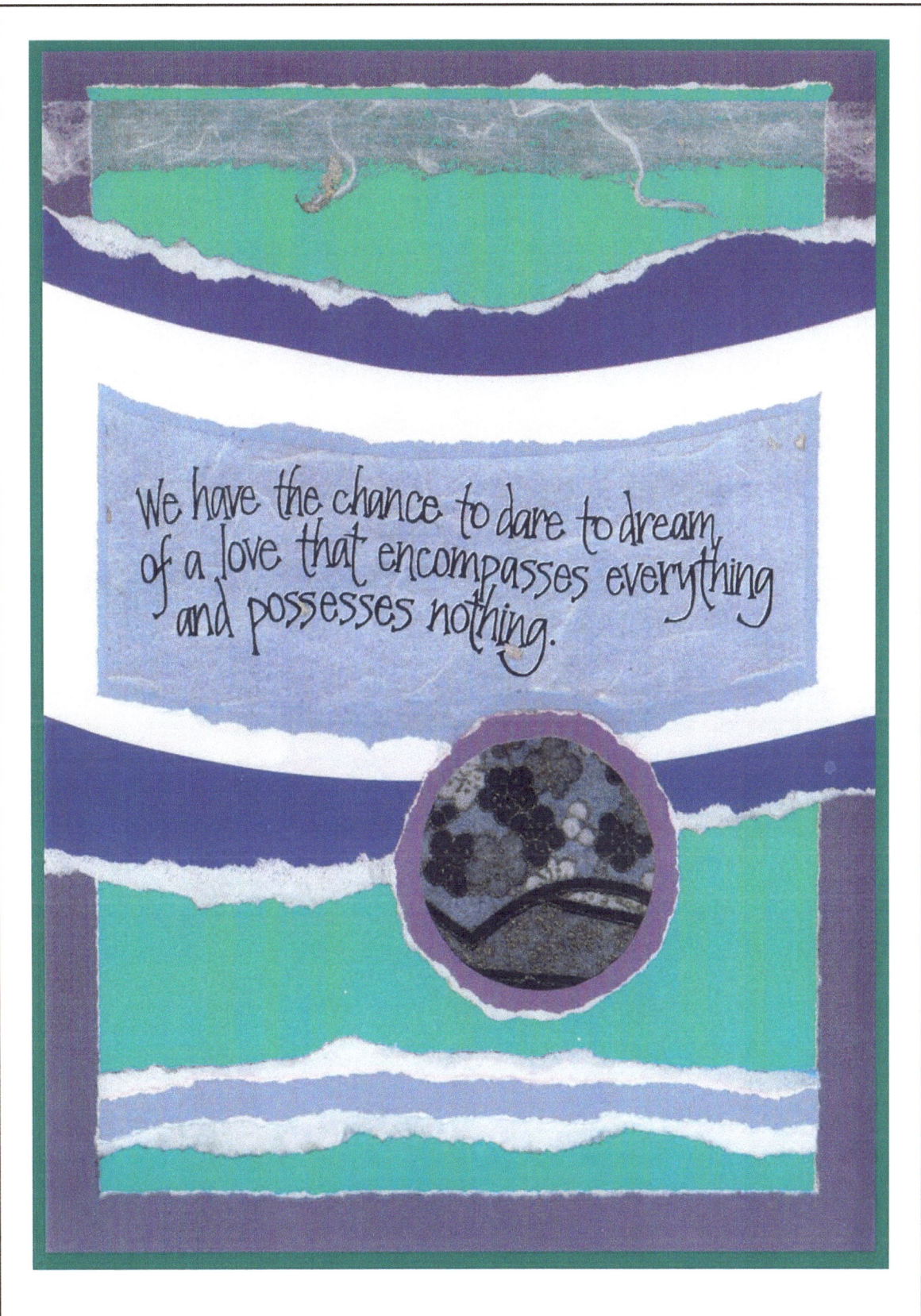

We have the chance to dare to dream of a love that encompasses everything and possesses nothing.

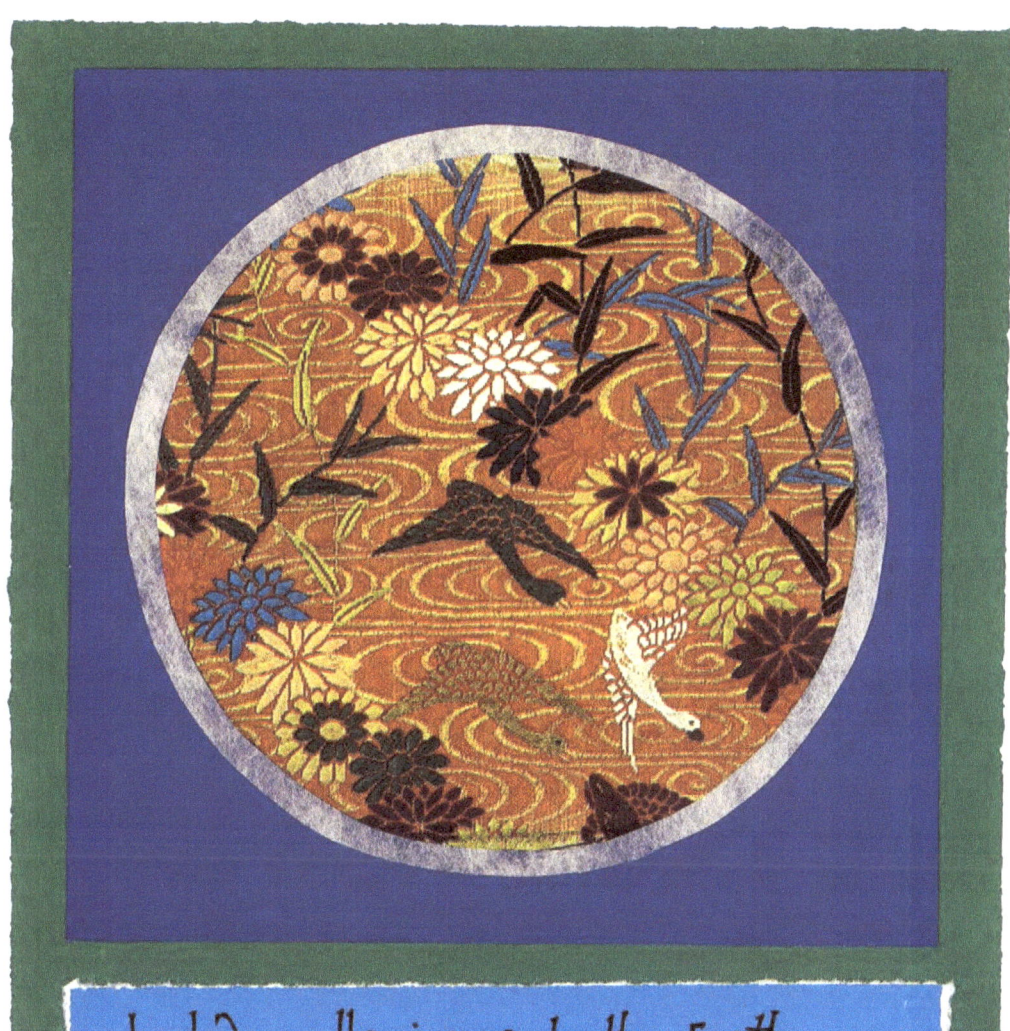

I pledge allegiance to the Earth,
and to the flora, fauna, and human life
that it supports, one planet, indivisible,
with safe air, water and soil
economic justice, equal rights
and peace for all.

Women's Environment and Development Organization

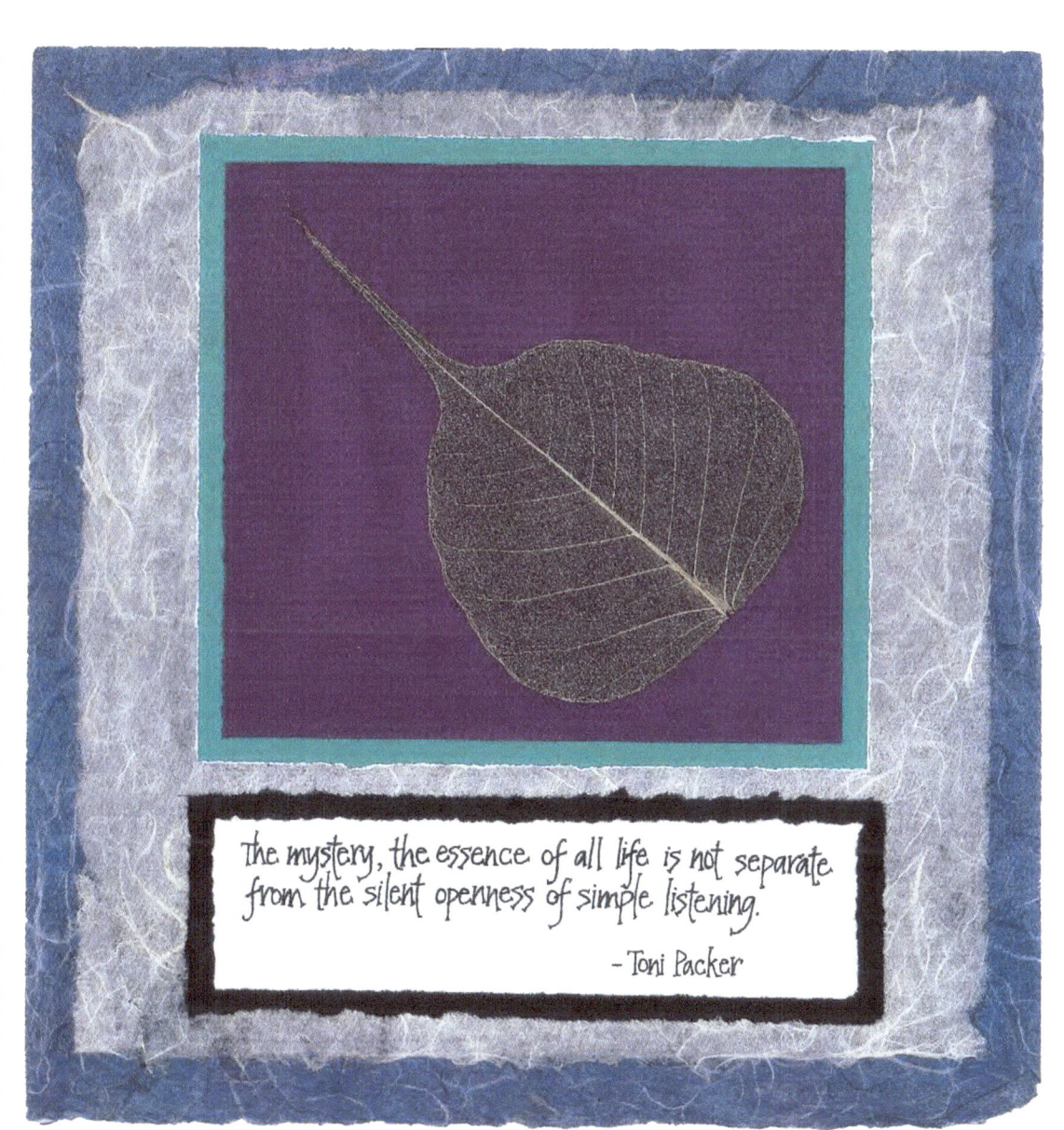

the mystery, the essence of all life is not separate from the silent openness of simple listening.

- Toni Packer

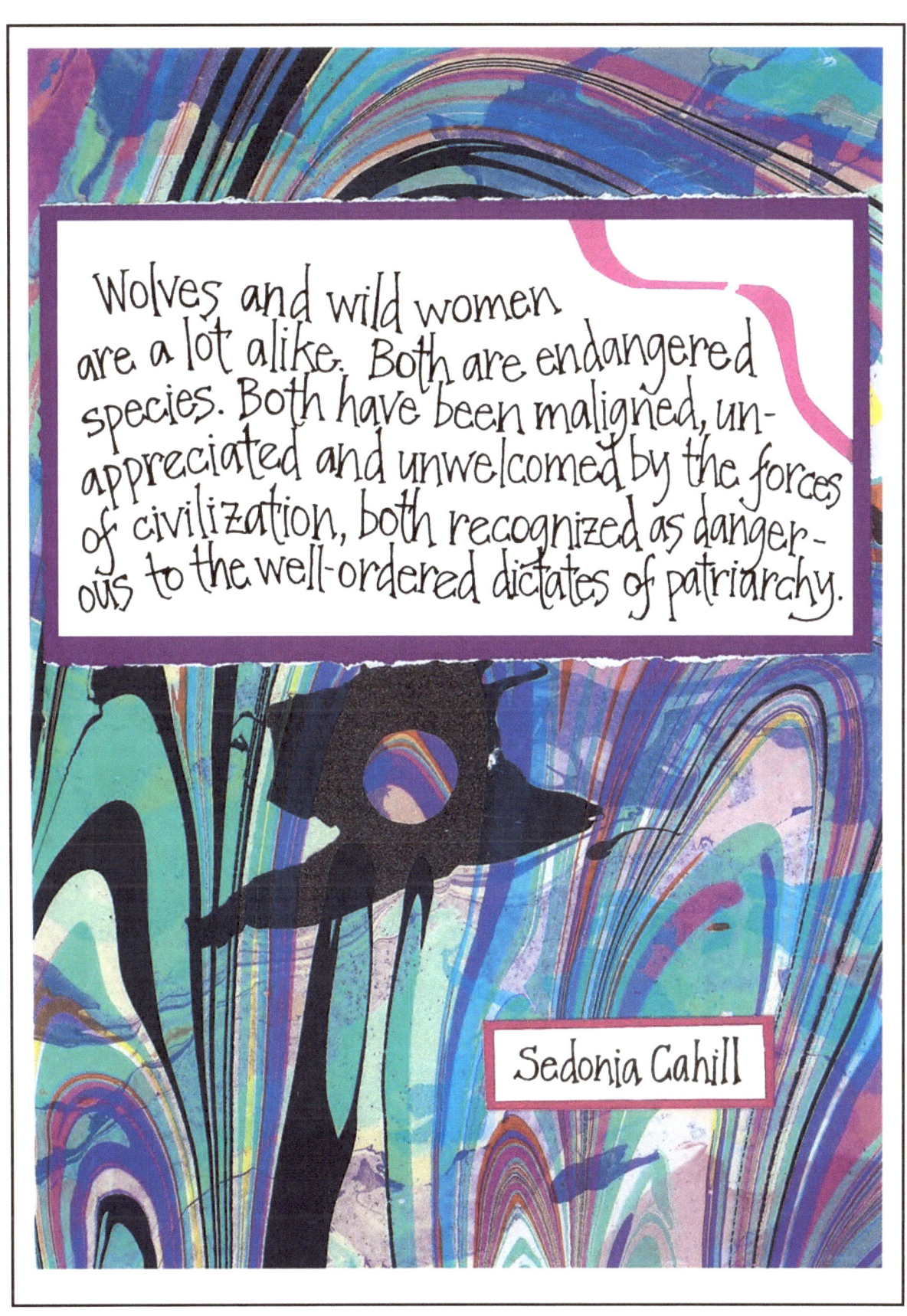

Wolves and wild women are a lot alike. Both are endangered species. Both have been maligned, unappreciated and unwelcomed by the forces of civilization, both recognized as dangerous to the well-ordered dictates of patriarchy.

Sedonia Cahill

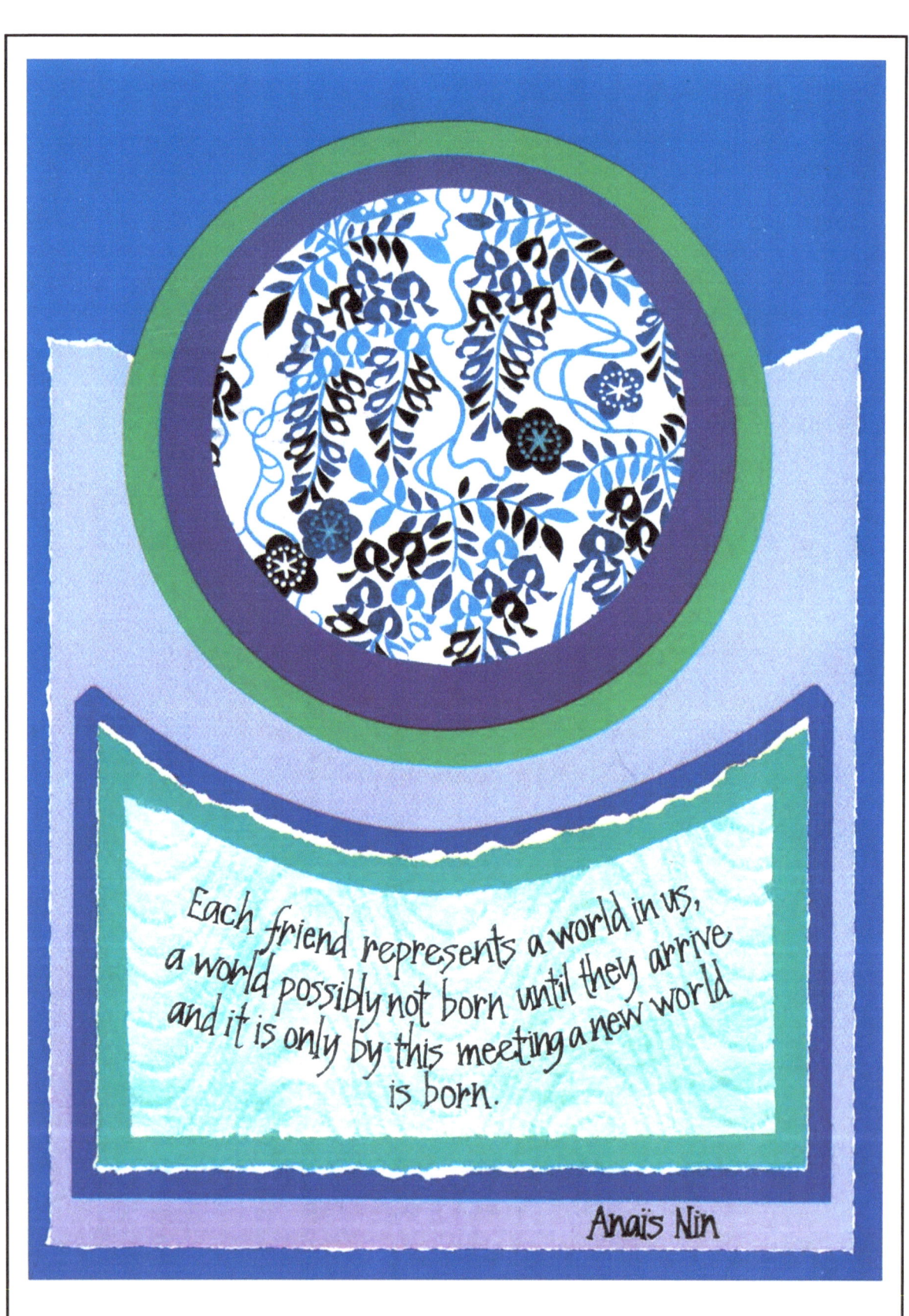

Each friend represents a world in us,
a world possibly not born until they arrive
and it is only by this meeting a new world
is born.

Anaïs Nin

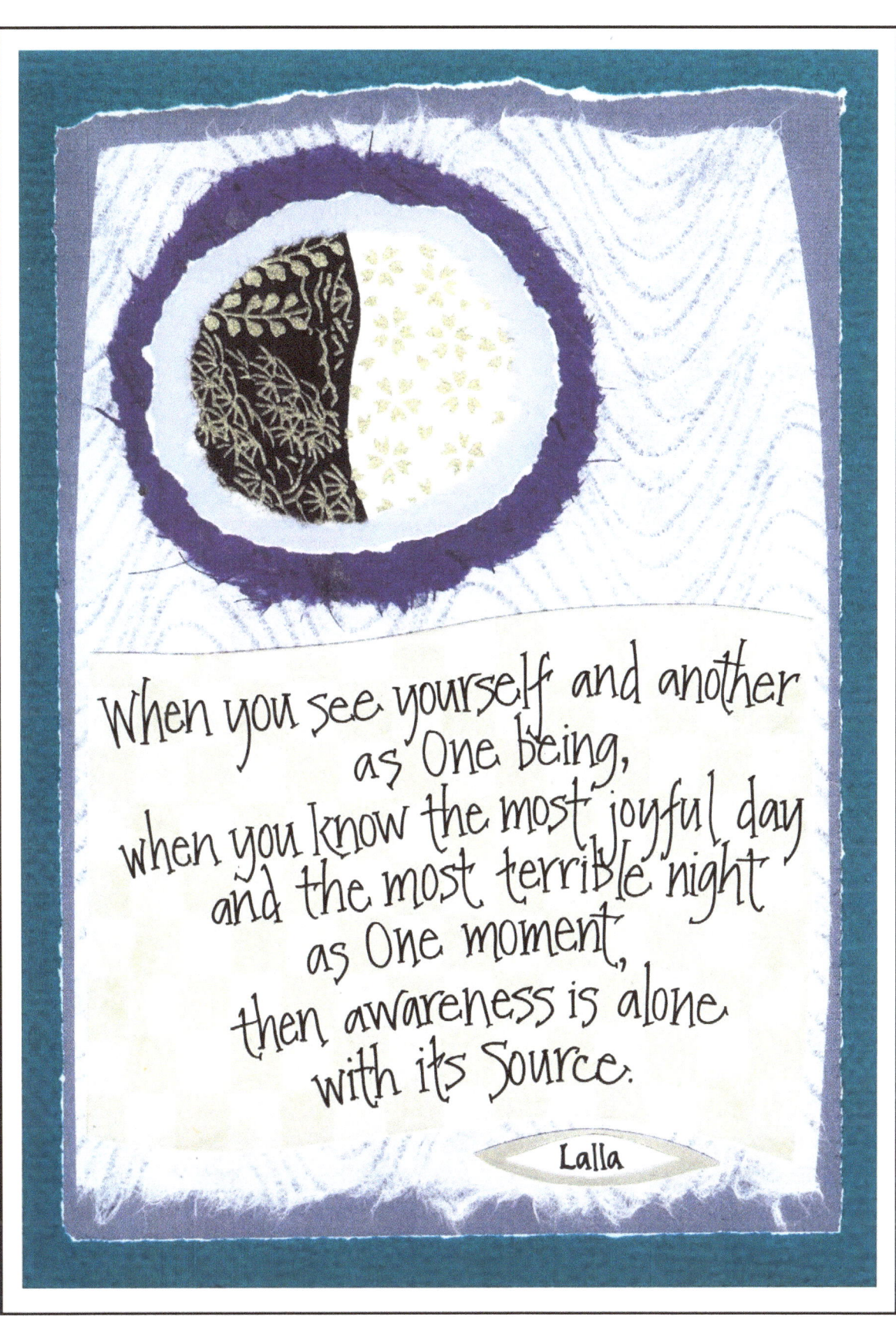

When you see yourself and another
as One being,
when you know the most joyful day
and the most terrible night
as One moment,
then awareness is alone
with its Source.

Lalla

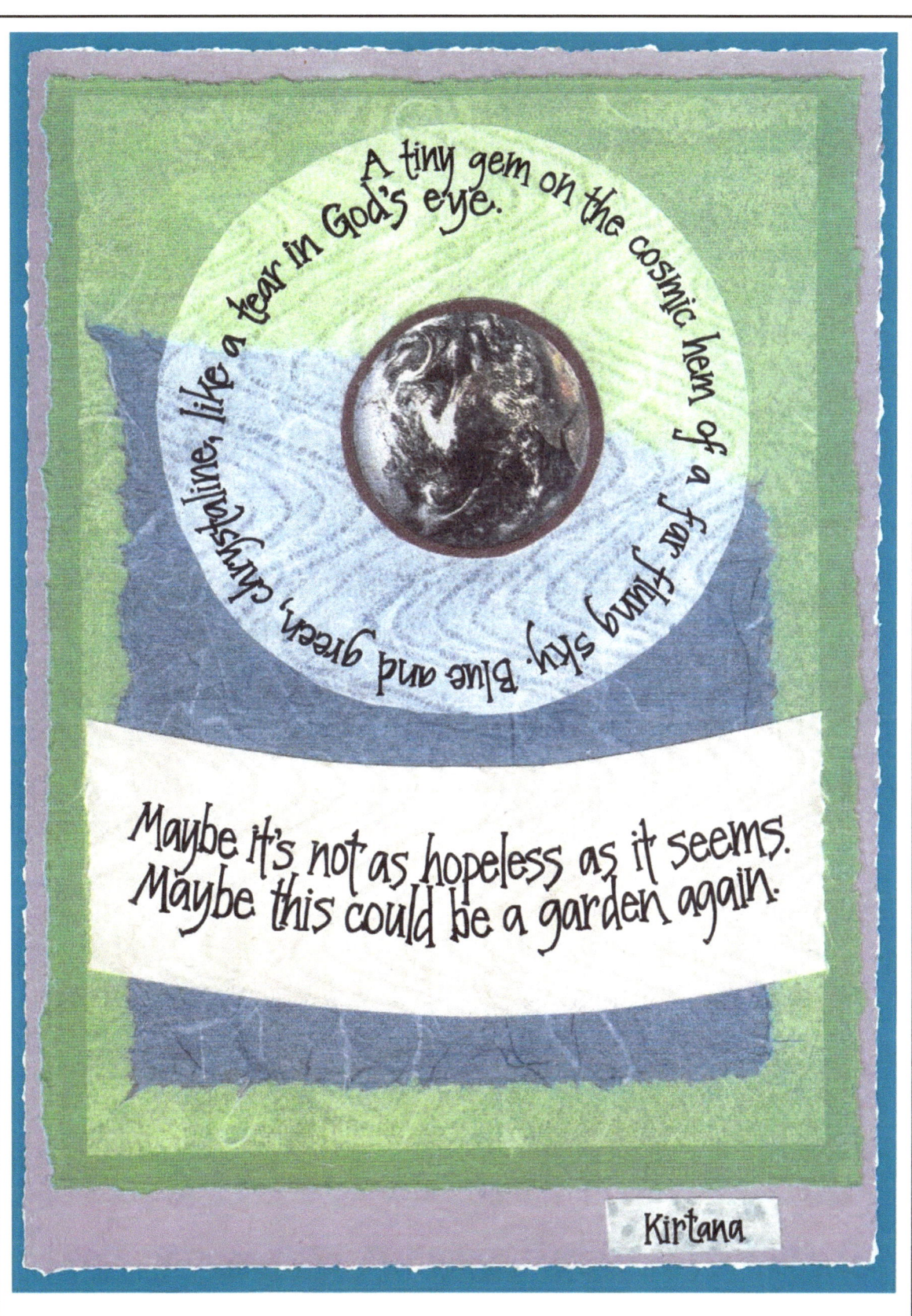

A tiny gem on the cosmic hem of a far flung sky. Blue and green, crystalline, like a tear in God's eye.

Maybe it's not as hopeless as it seems. Maybe this could be a garden again.

Kirtana

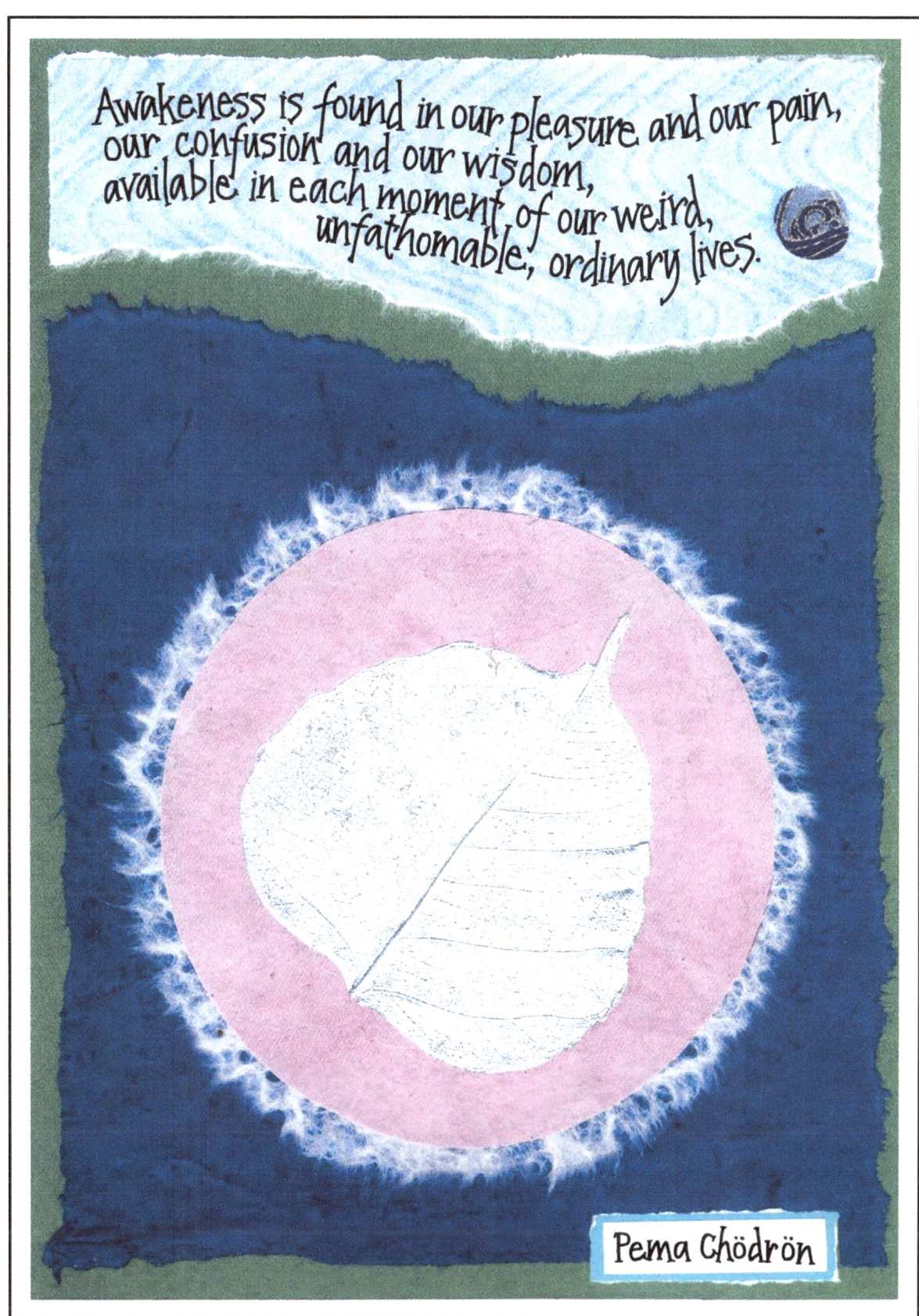

Awakeness is found in our pleasure and our pain, our confusion and our wisdom, available in each moment of our weird, unfathomable, ordinary lives.

Pema Chödrön

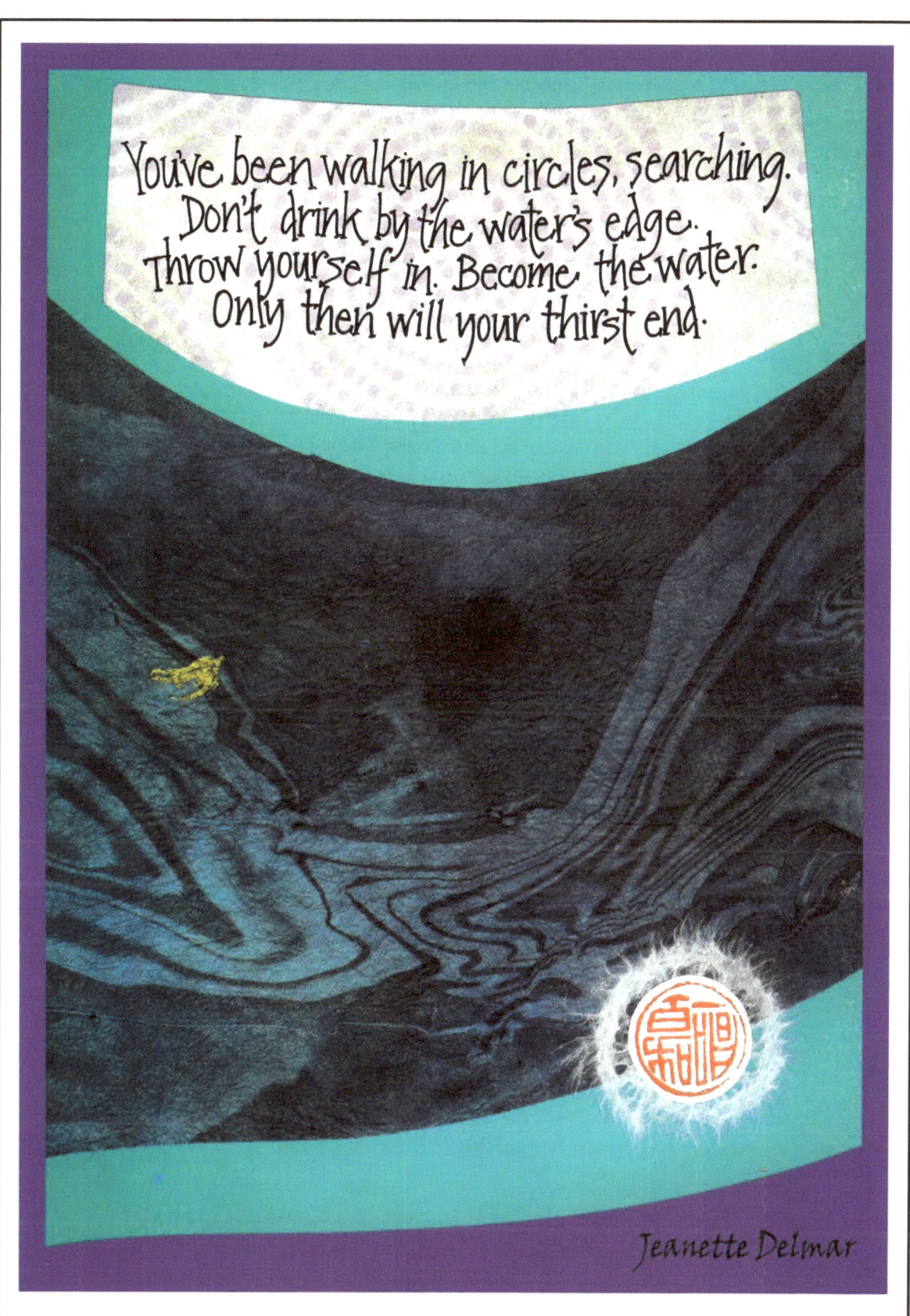

You've been walking in circles, searching.
Don't drink by the water's edge.
Throw yourself in. Become the water.
Only then will your thirst end.

Jeanette Delmar

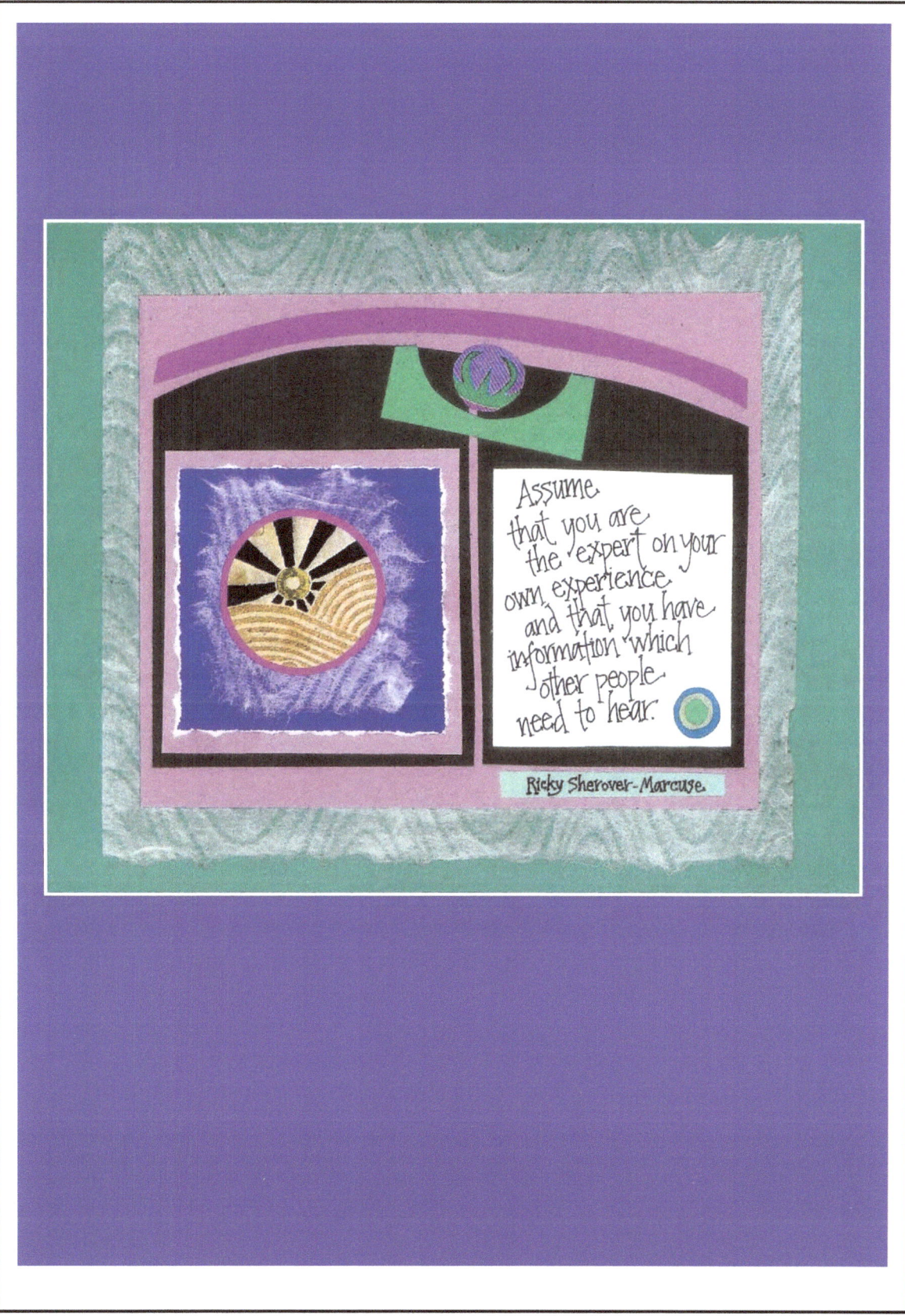

Assume
that you are
the expert on your
own experience
and that you have
information which
other people
need to hear.

Ricky Sherover-Marcuse.

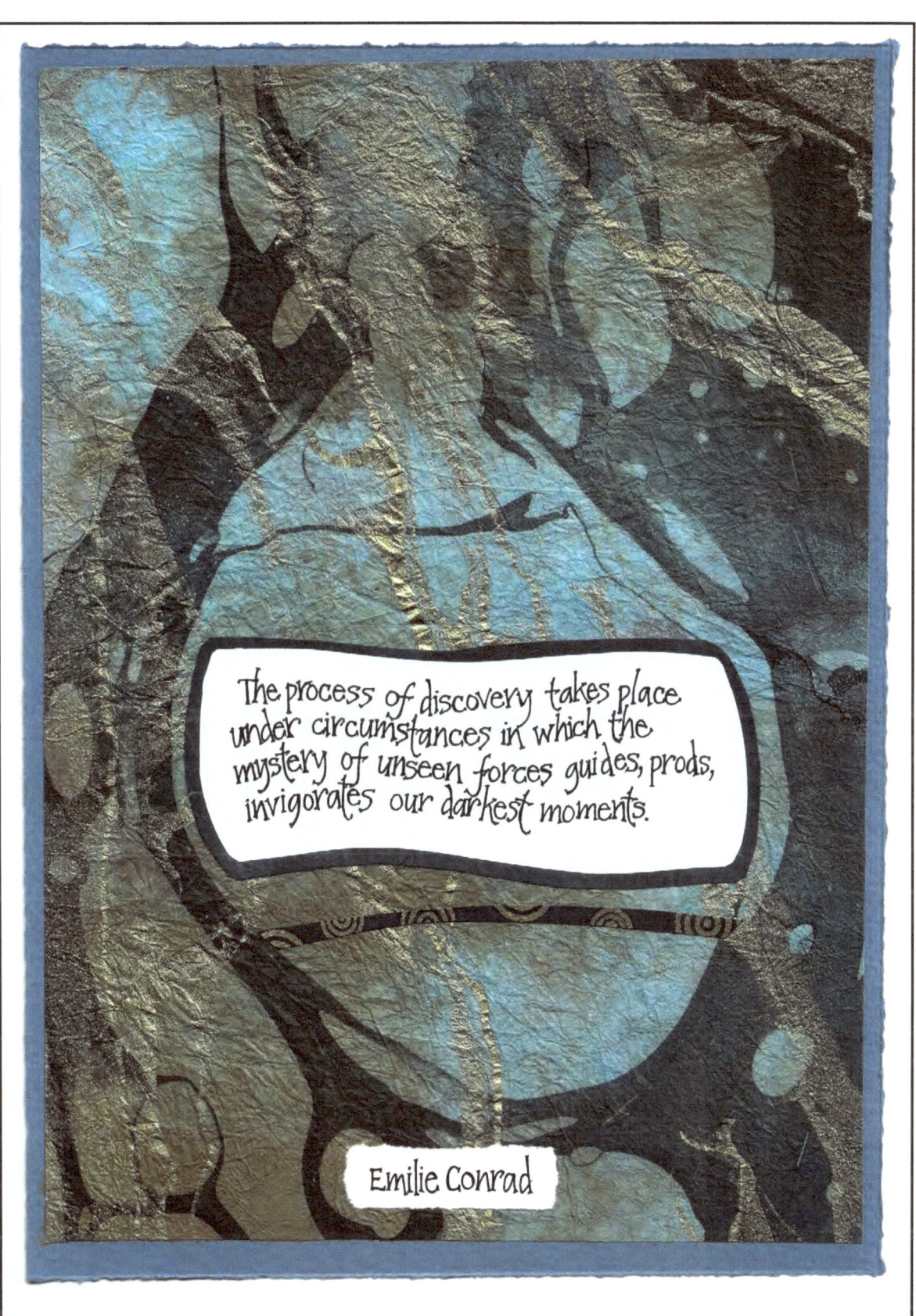

The process of discovery takes place under circumstances in which the mystery of unseen forces guides, prods, invigorates our darkest moments.

Emilie Conrad

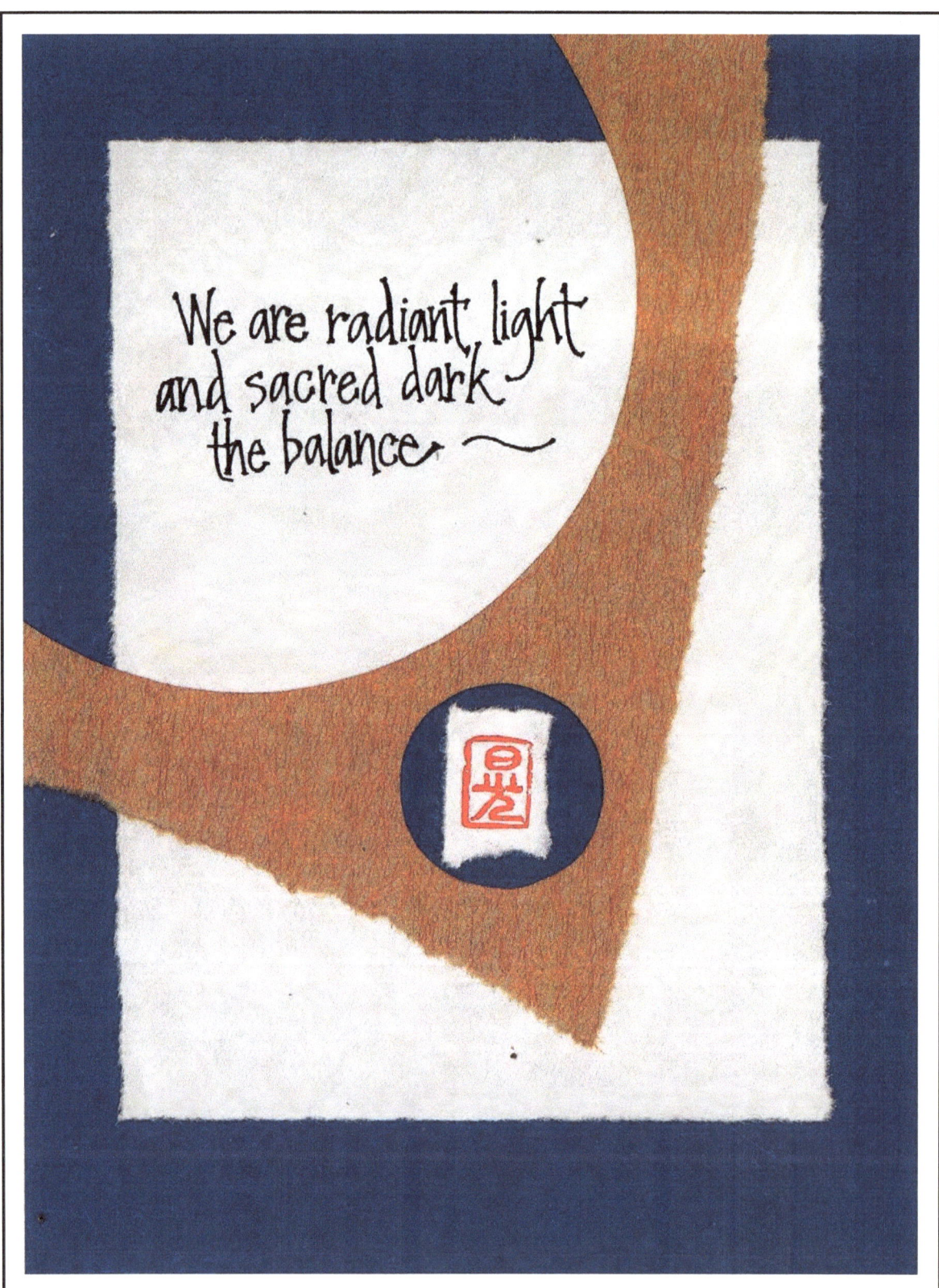

We are radiant light
and sacred dark
the balance

Starhawk

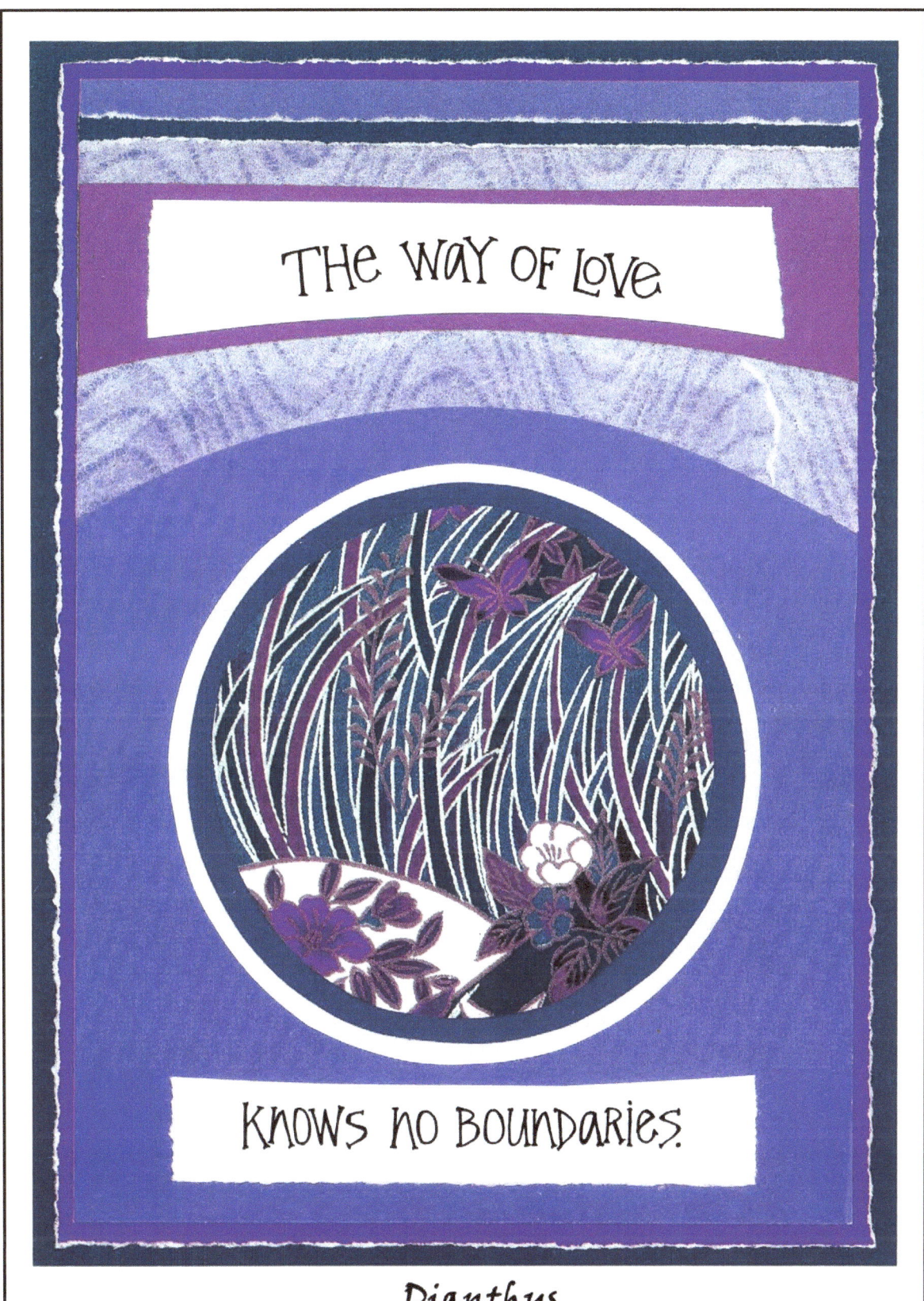

THE WAY OF LOVE

KNOWS NO BOUNDARIES.

Dianthus

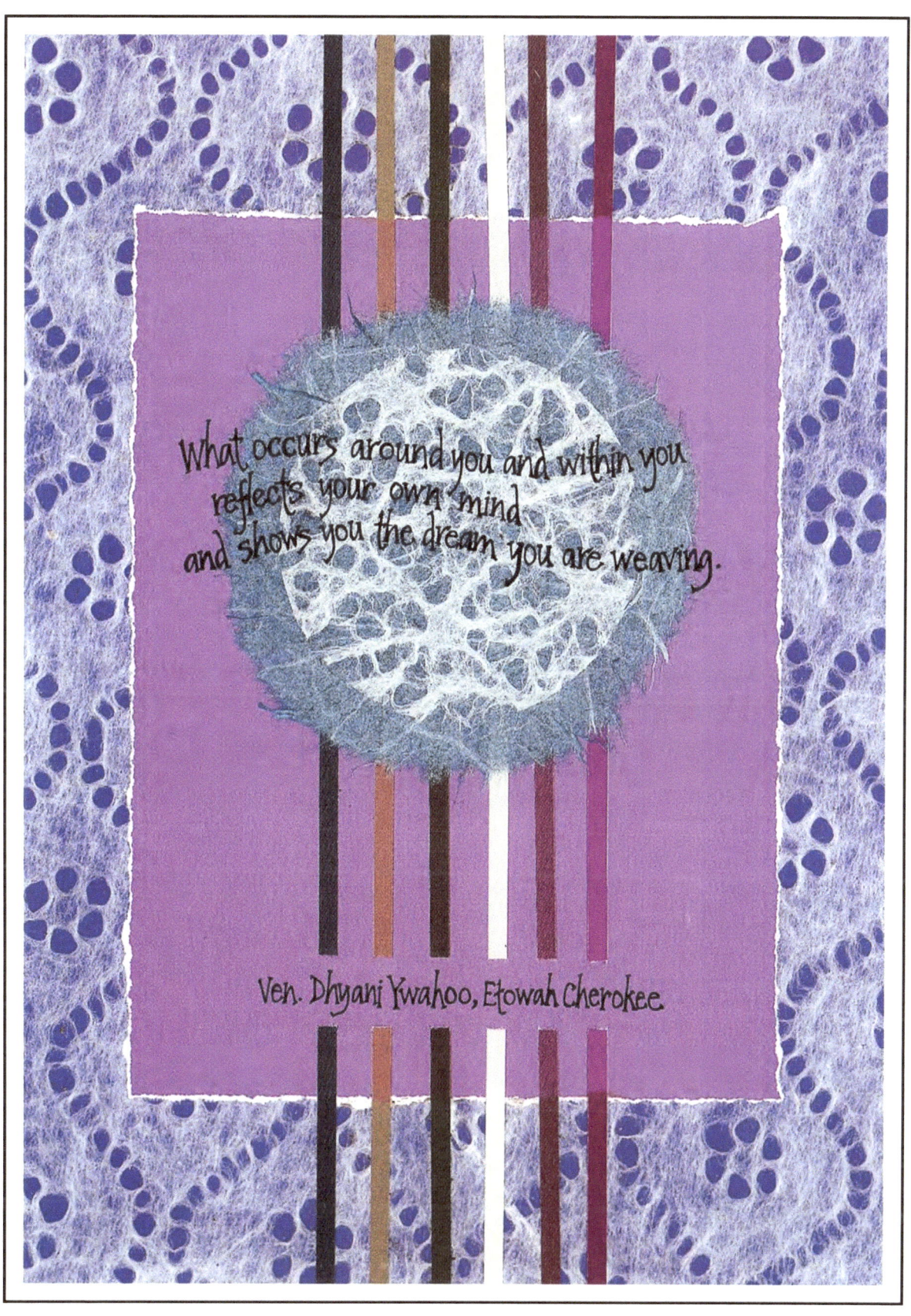

What occurs around you and within you
reflects your own mind
and shows you the dream you are weaving.

Ven. Dhyani Ywahoo, Etowah Cherokee

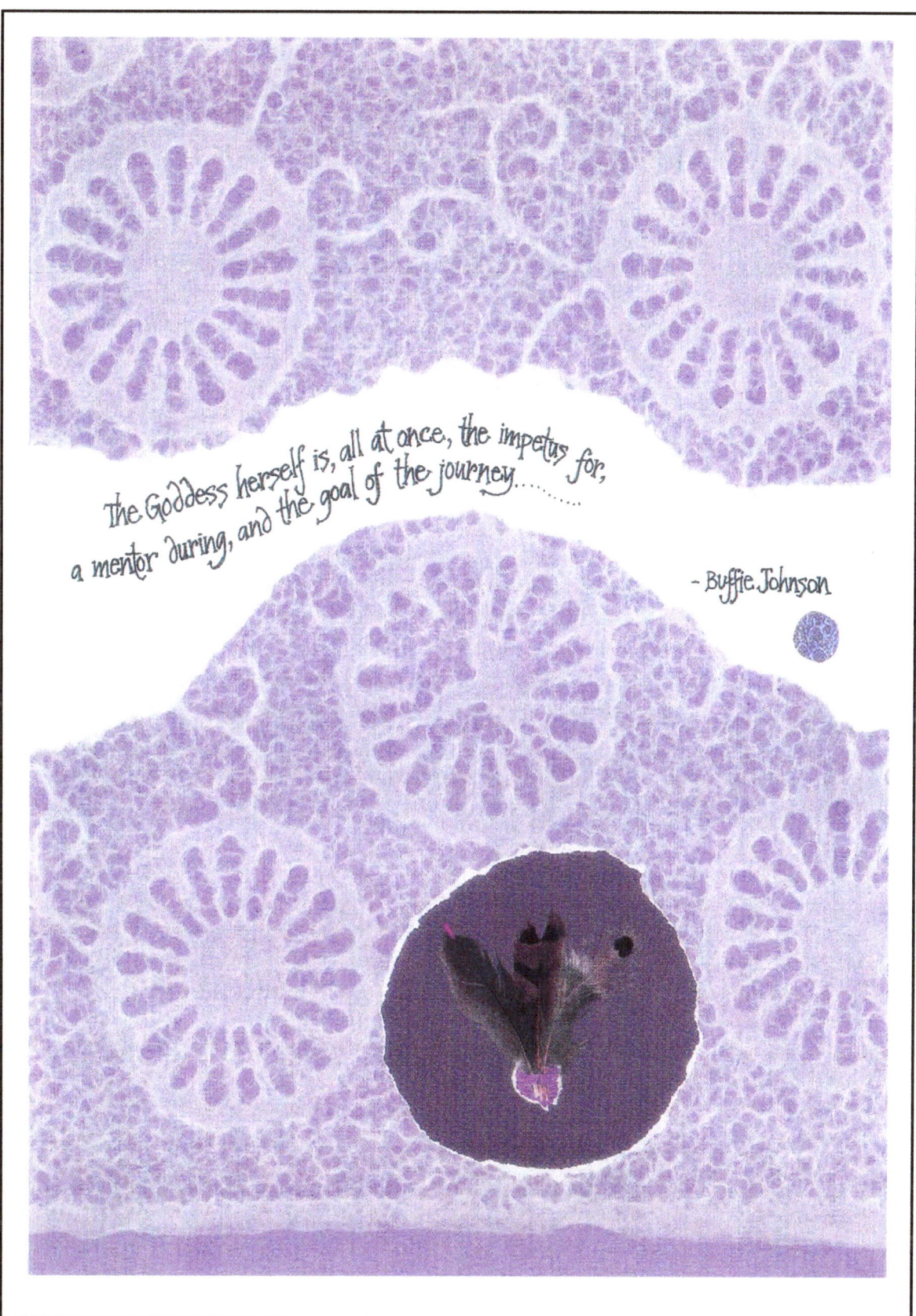

The Goddess herself is, all at once, the impetus for, a mentor during, and the goal of the journey..........

– Buffie Johnson

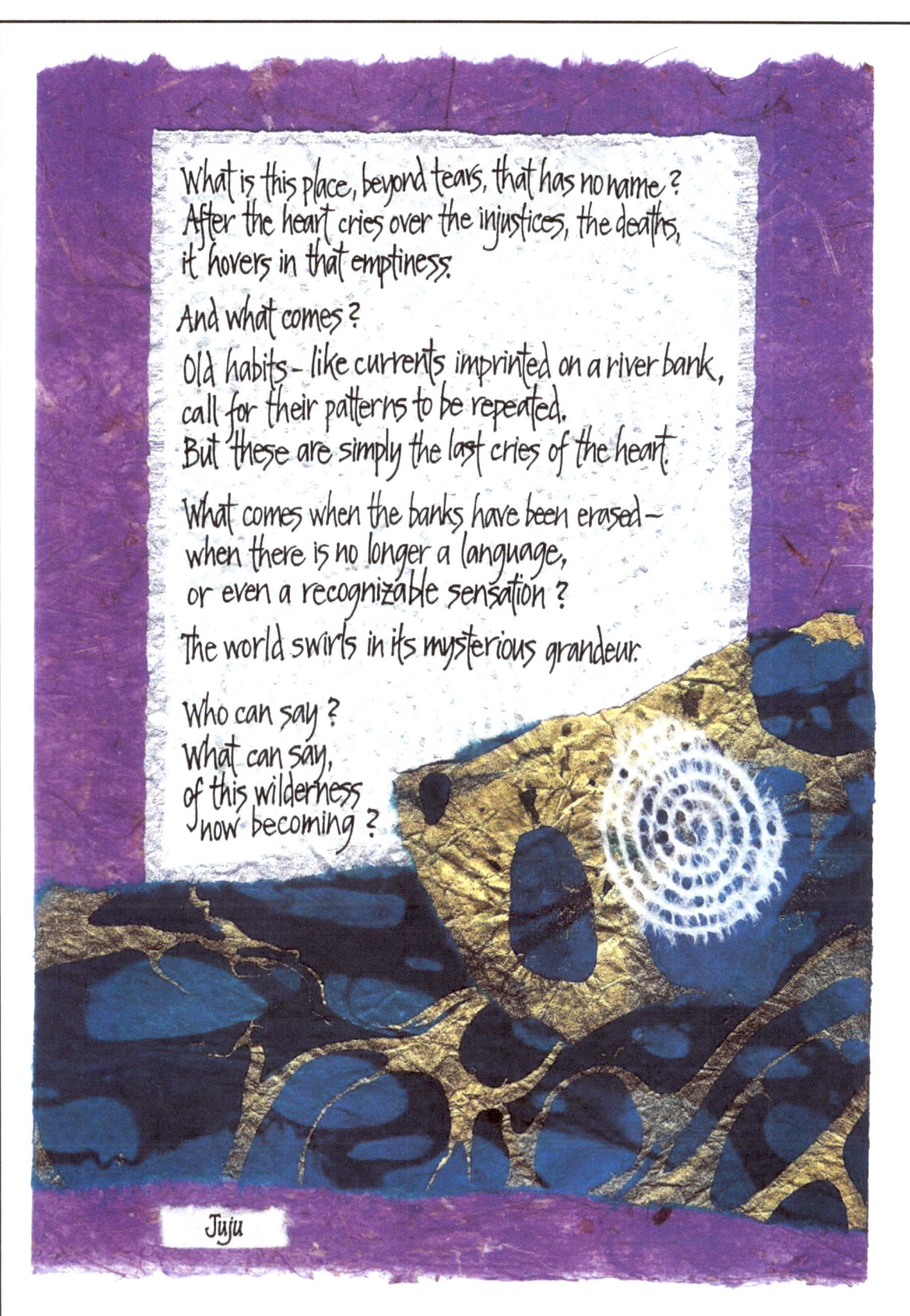

What is this place, beyond tears, that has no name?
After the heart cries over the injustices, the deaths,
it hovers in that emptiness.

And what comes?

Old habits - like currents imprinted on a river bank,
call for their patterns to be repeated.
But these are simply the last cries of the heart.

What comes when the banks have been erased -
when there is no longer a language,
or even a recognizable sensation?

The world swirls in its mysterious grandeur.

Who can say?
What can say,
of this wilderness
now becoming?

Juju

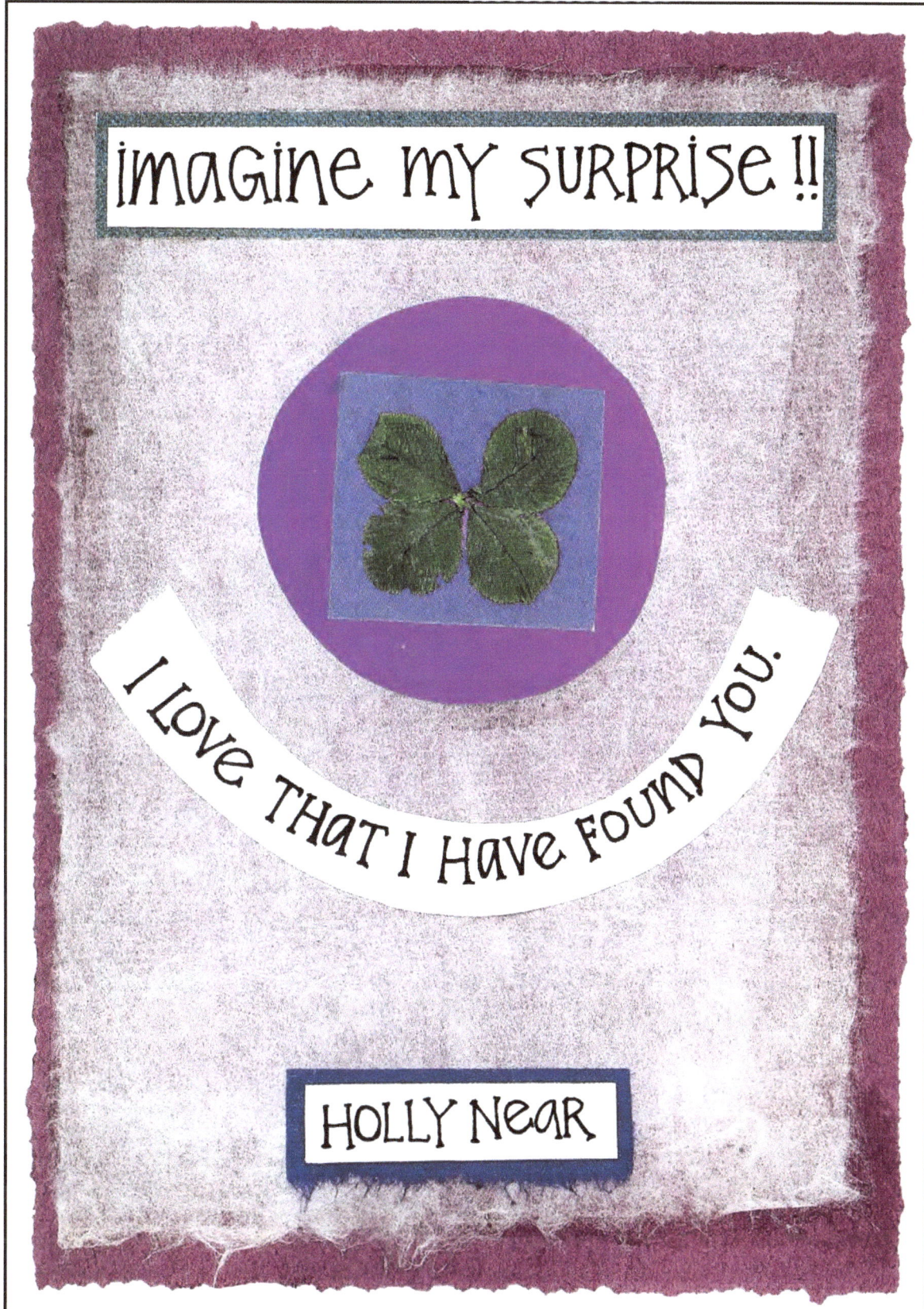

imagine my surprise !!

I love that I have found you.

Holly Near

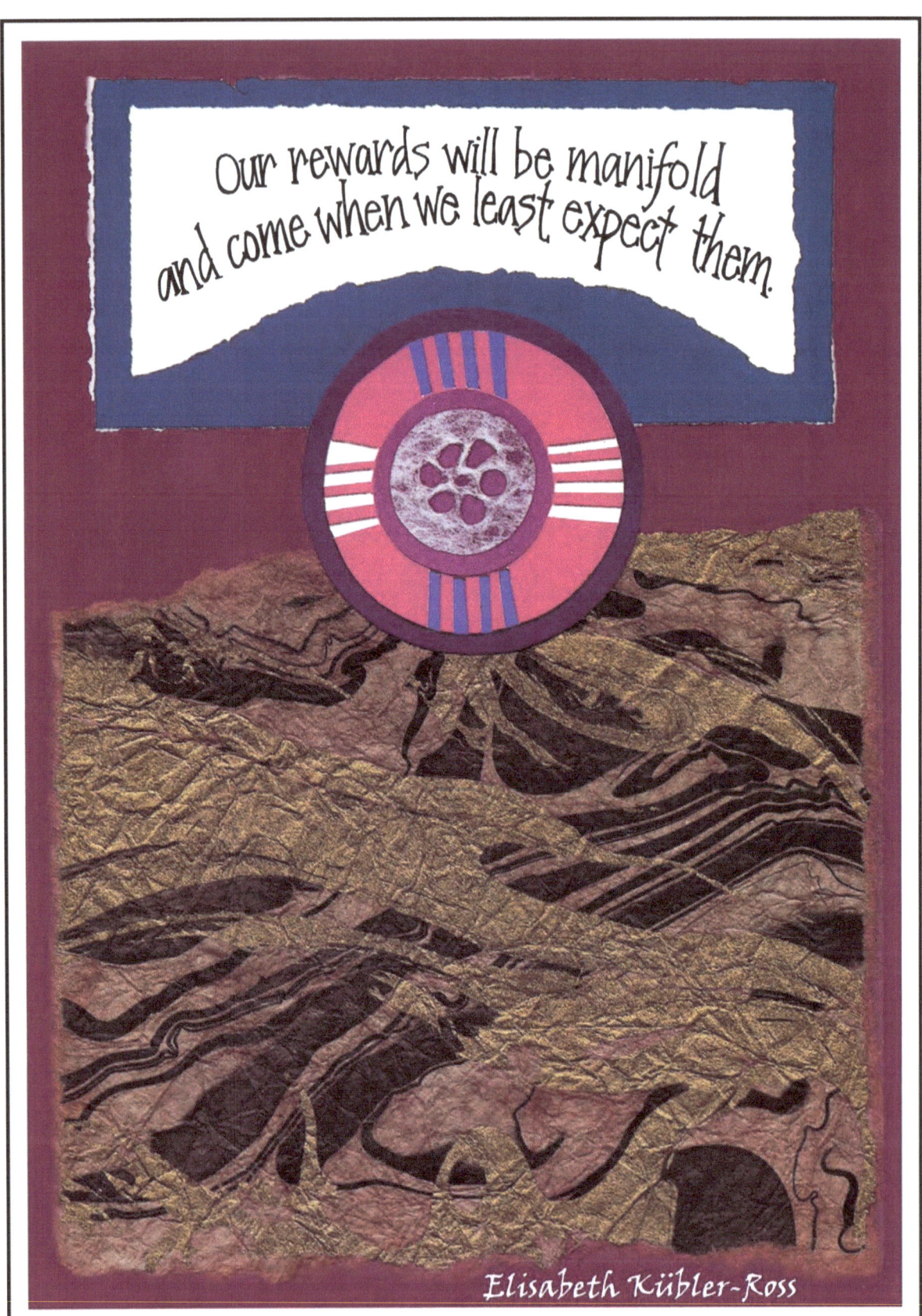

Our rewards will be manifold and come when we least expect them.

Elisabeth Kübler-Ross

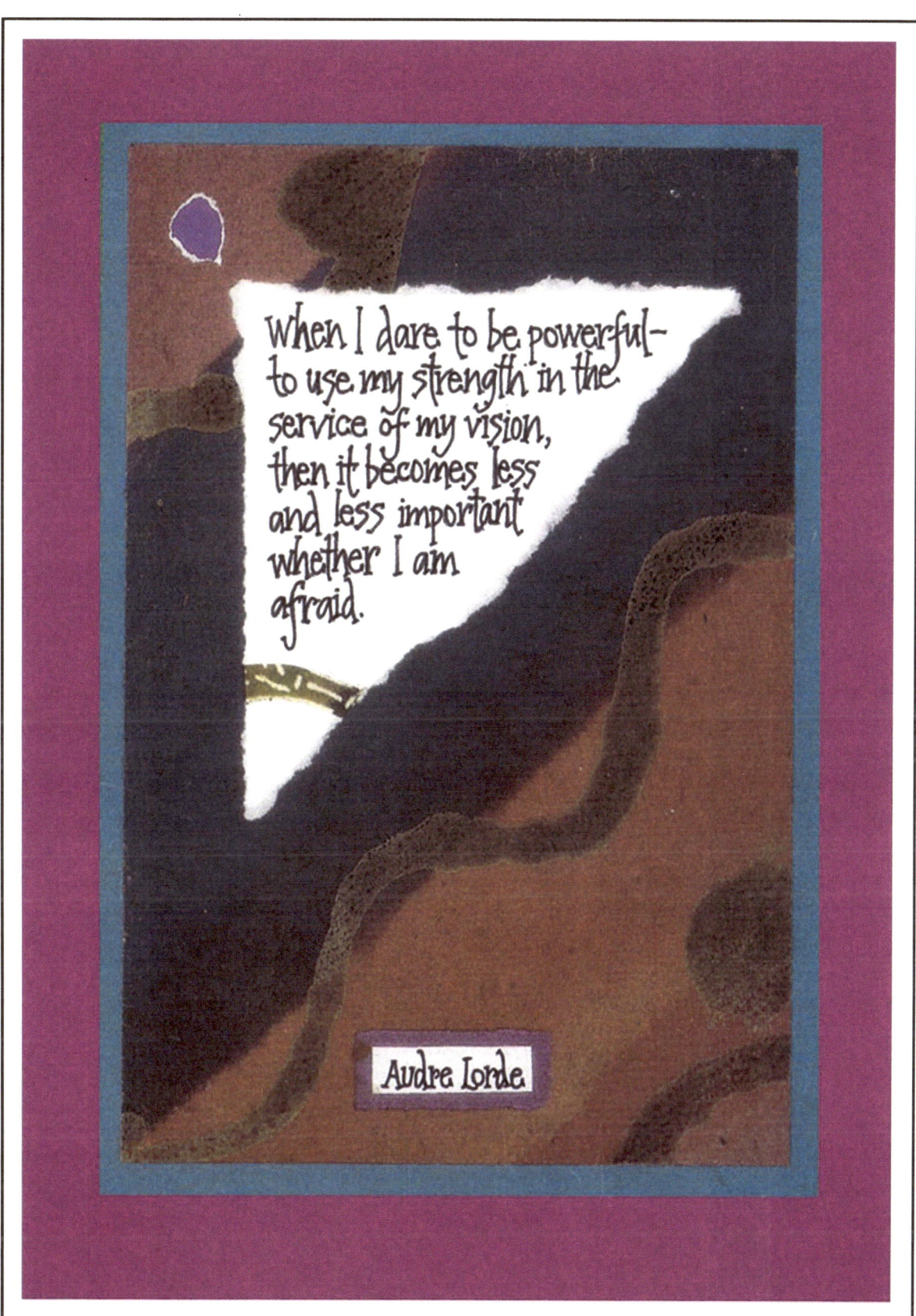

When I dare to be powerful—
to use my strength in the
service of my vision,
then it becomes less
and less important
whether I am
afraid.

Audre Lorde

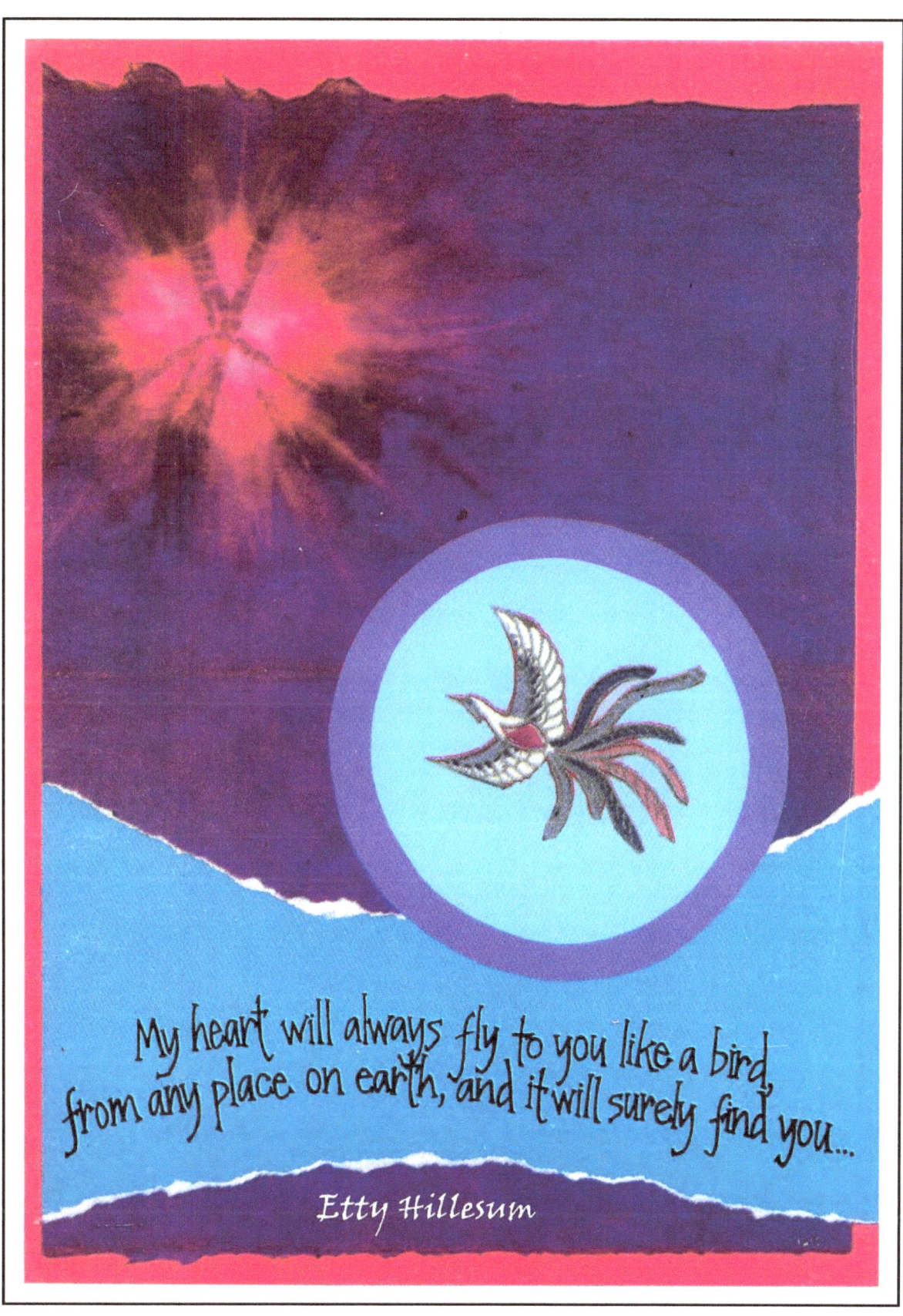

My heart will always fly to you like a bird, from any place on earth, and it will surely find you...

Etty Hillesum

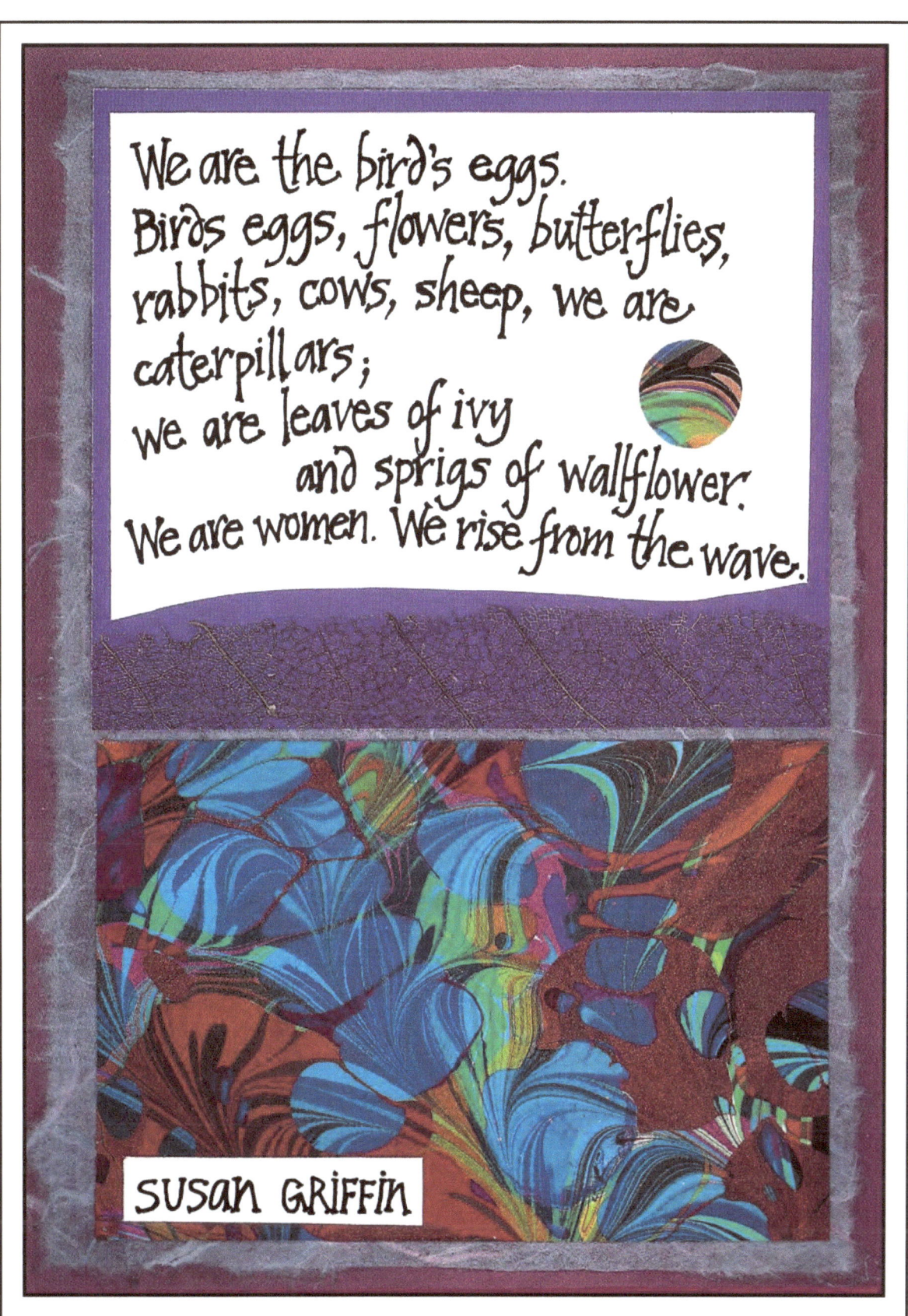

We are the bird's eggs.
Birds eggs, flowers, butterflies,
rabbits, cows, sheep, we are
caterpillars;
we are leaves of ivy
            and sprigs of wallflower.
We are women. We rise from the wave.

SUSAN GRIFFIN

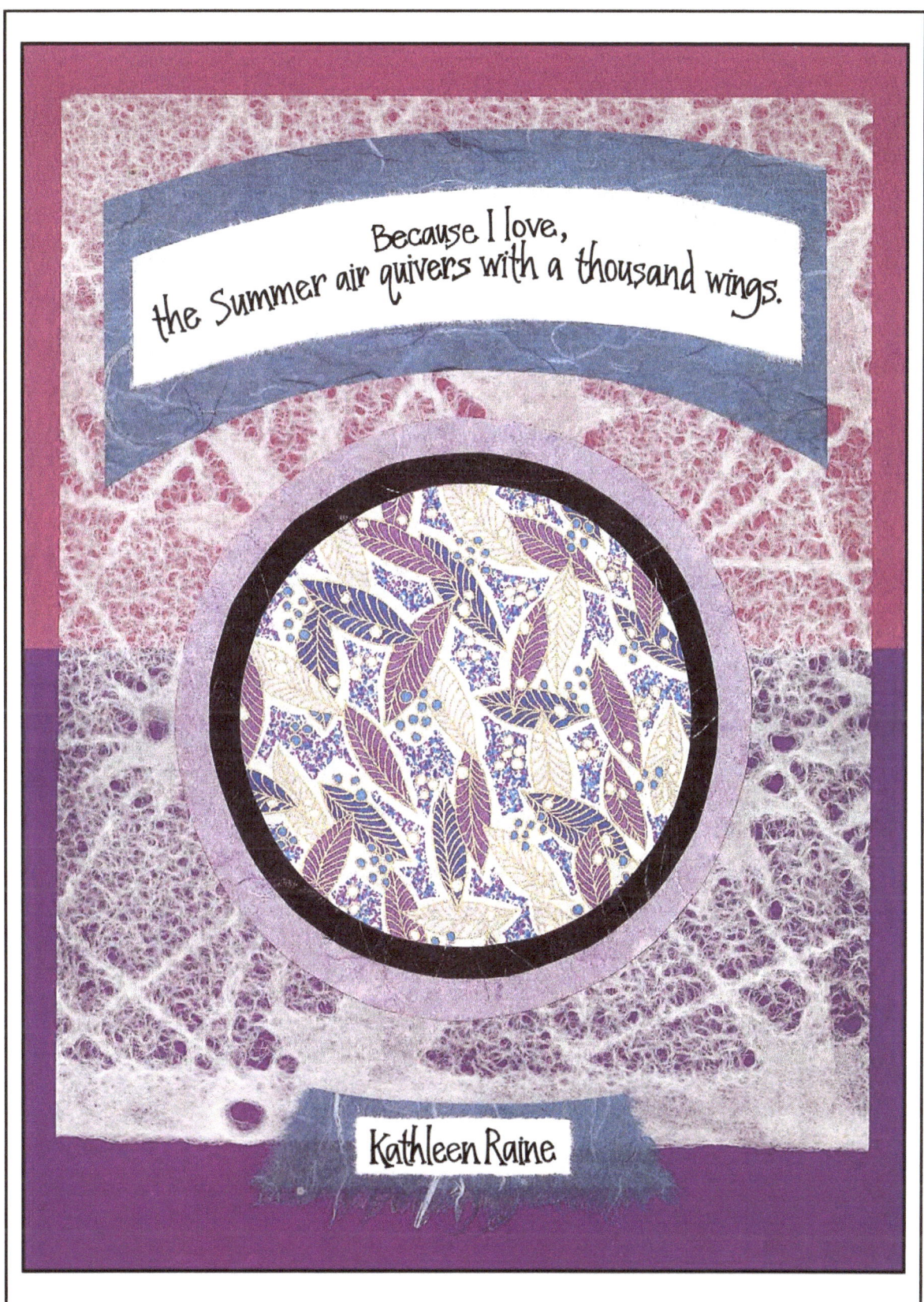

Because I love,
the Summer air quivers with a thousand wings.

Kathleen Raine

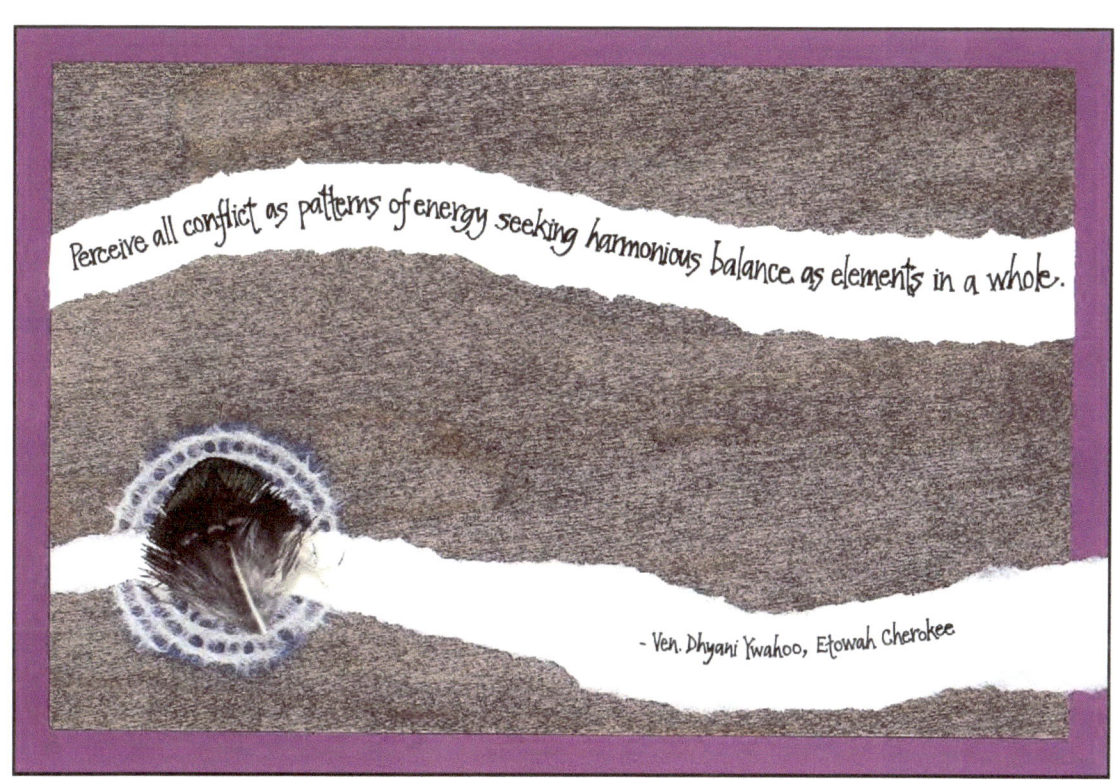

Perceive all conflict as patterns of energy seeking harmonious balance as elements in a whole.

– Ven. Dhyani Ywahoo, Etowah Cherokee

Practice random kindness

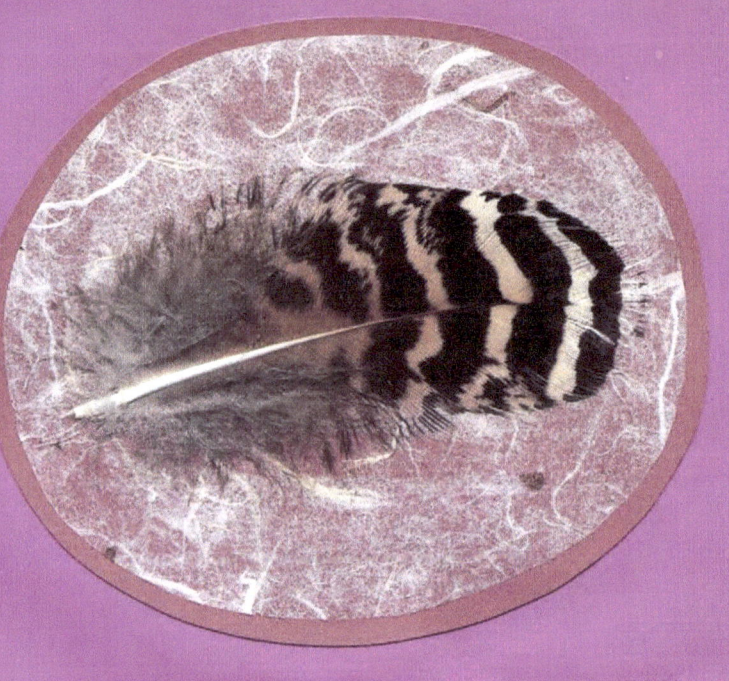

and senseless acts of Beauty.

Anne Herbert

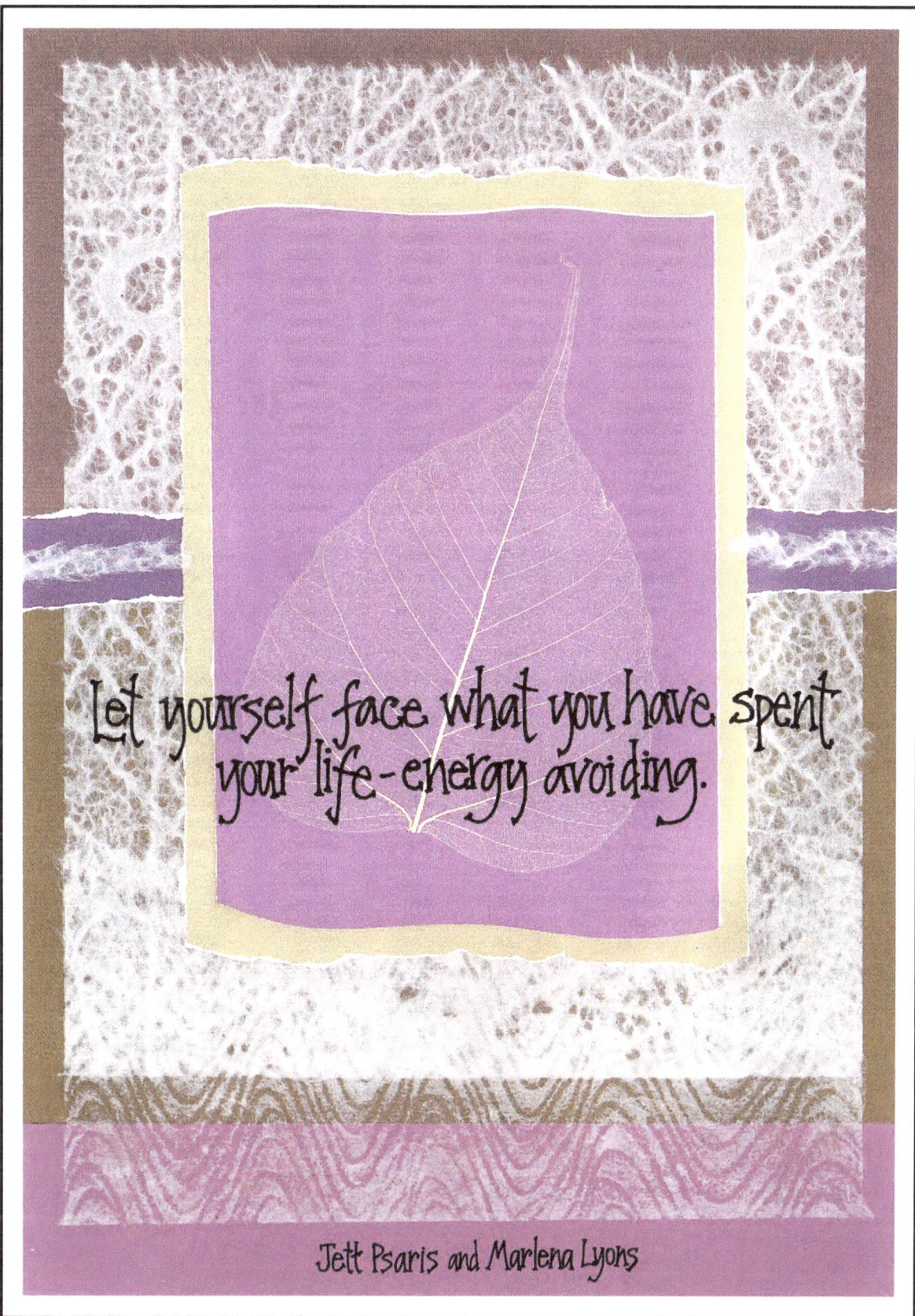

Let yourself face what you have spent your life-energy avoiding.

Jett Psaris and Marlena Lyons

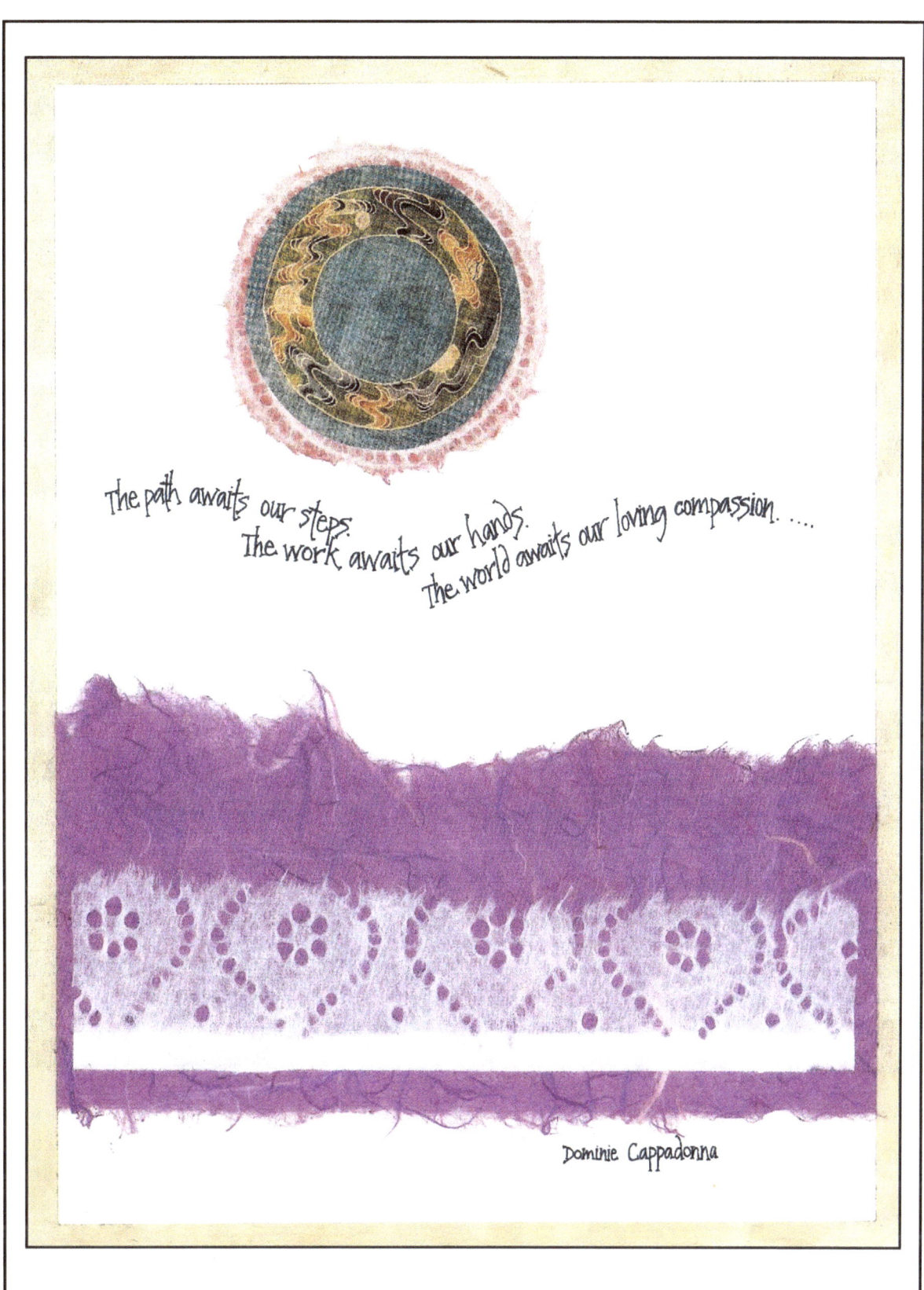

The path awaits our steps.
The work awaits our hands.
The world awaits our loving compassion. ....

Dominie Cappadonna

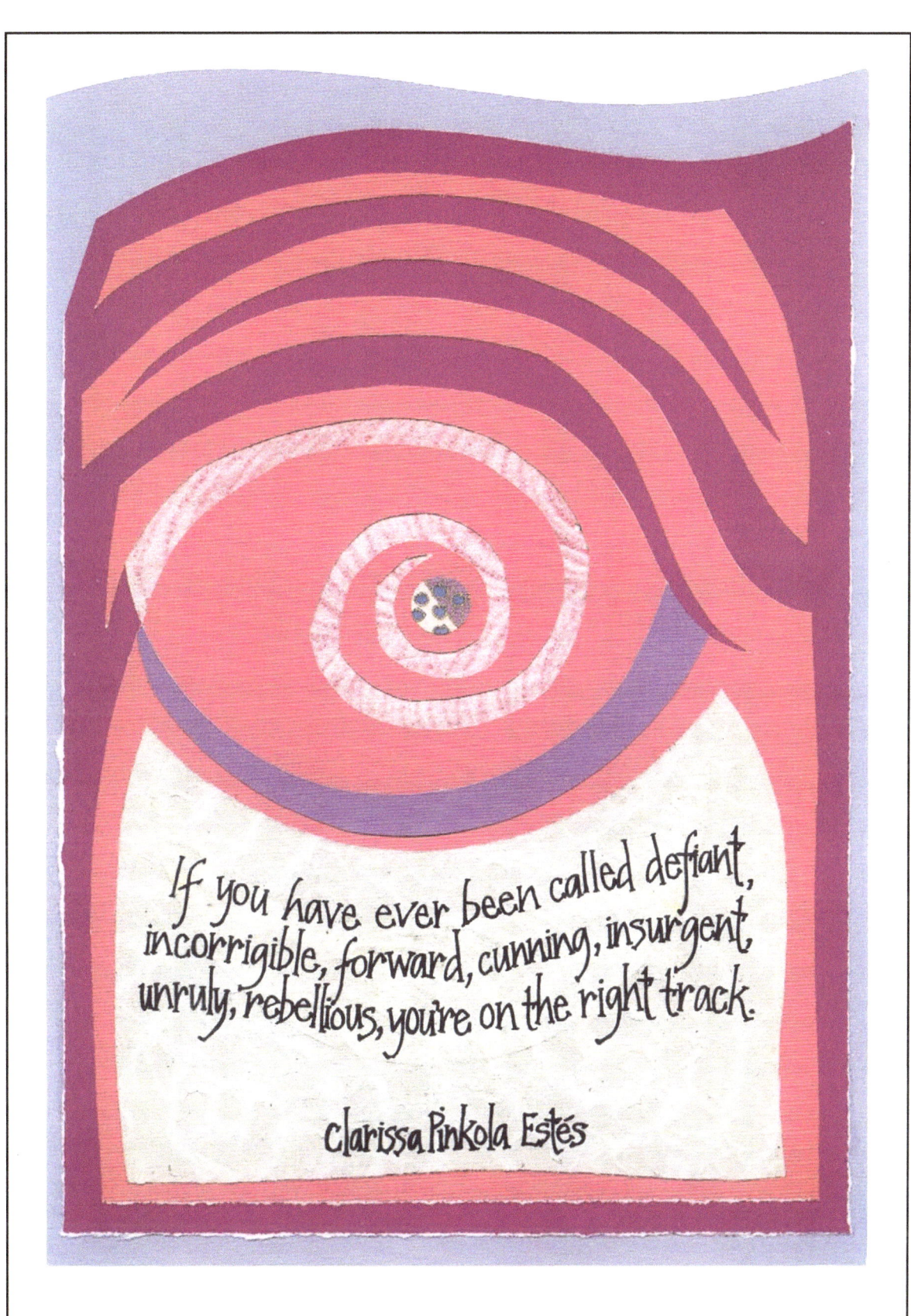

If you have ever been called defiant, incorrigible, forward, cunning, insurgent, unruly, rebellious, you're on the right track.

Clarissa Pinkola Estés

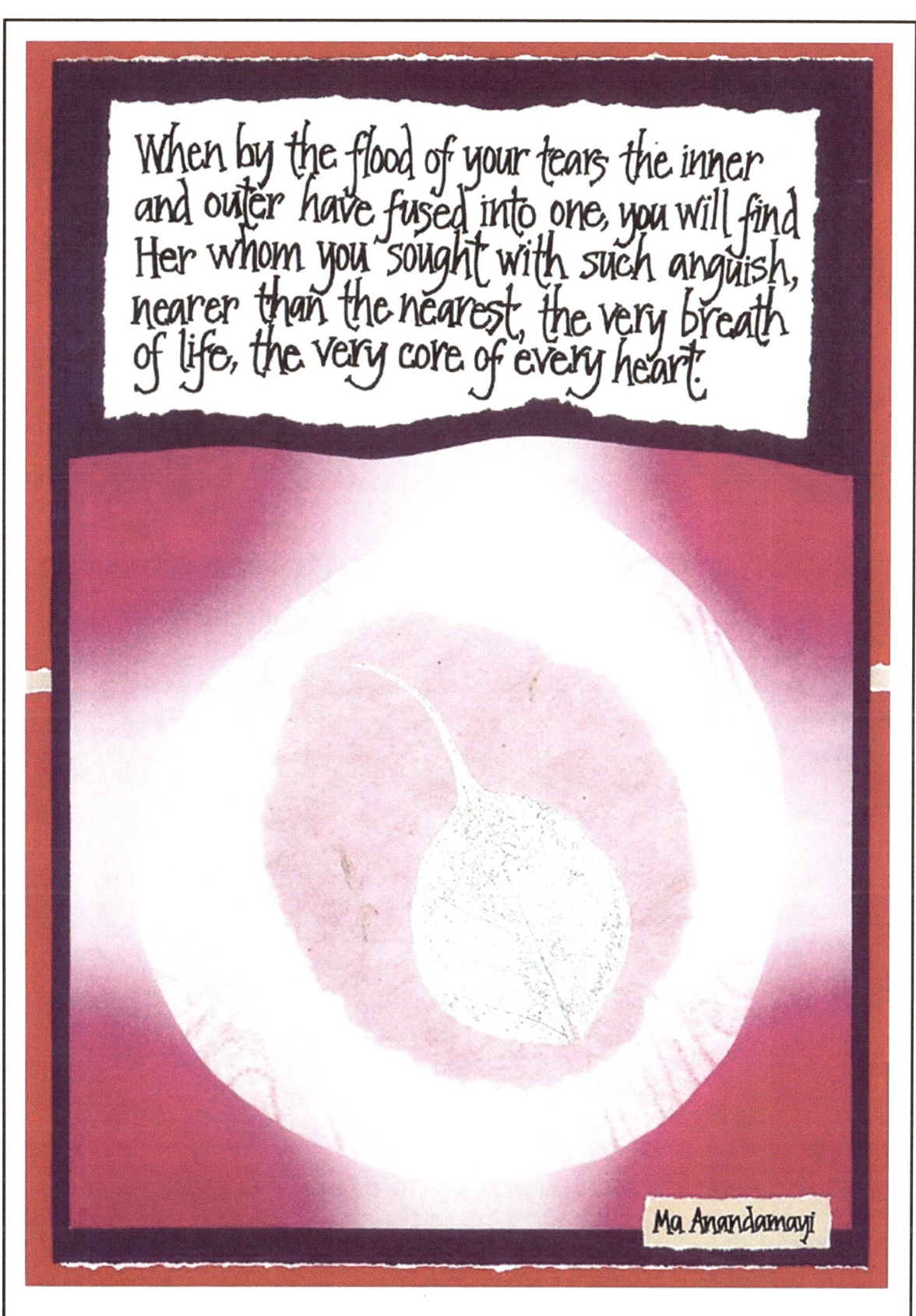

When by the flood of your tears the inner and outer have fused into one, you will find Her whom you sought with such anguish, nearer than the nearest, the very breath of life, the very core of every heart.

Ma Anandamayi

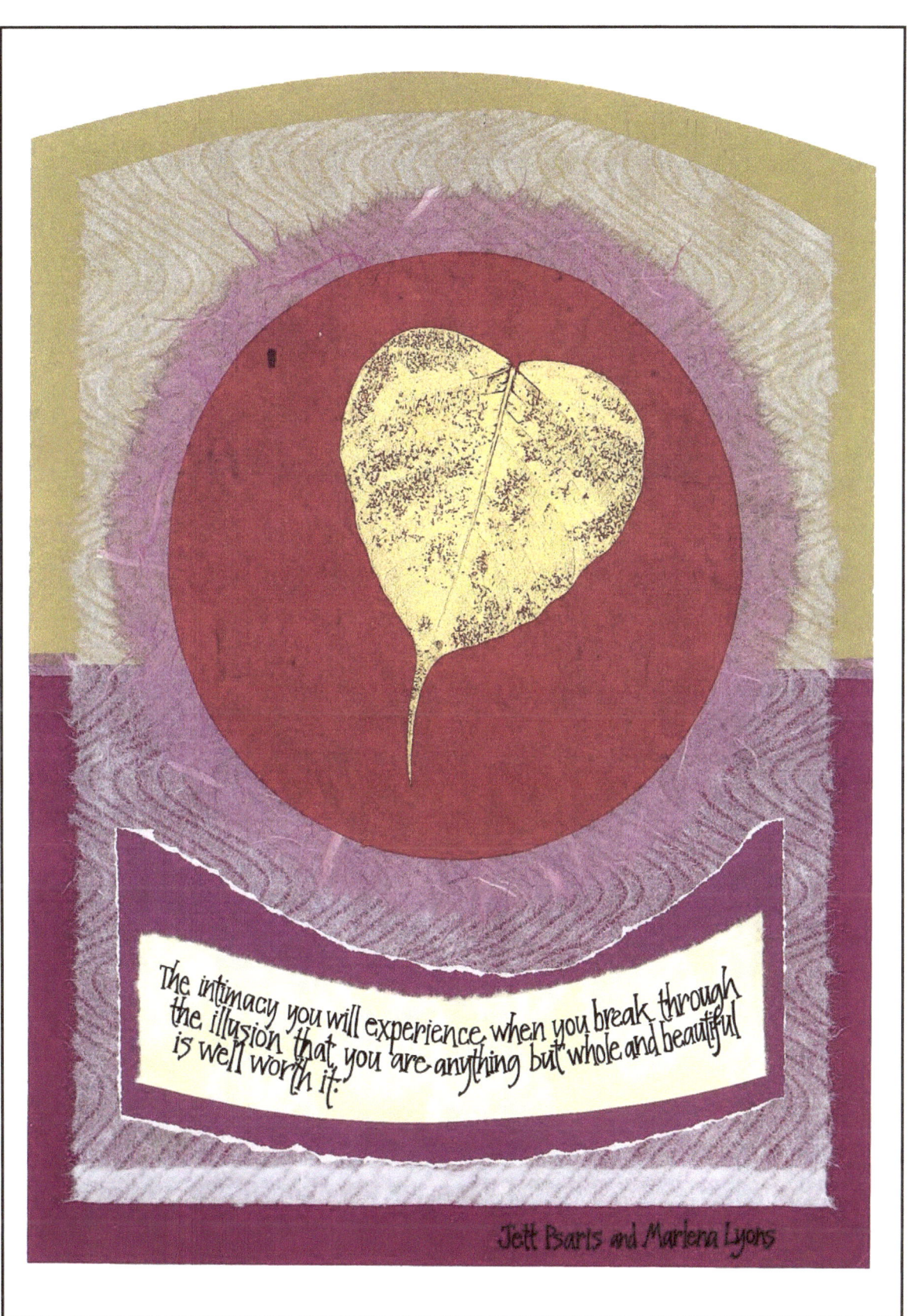

The intimacy you will experience when you break through the illusion that you are anything but whole and beautiful is well worth it.

Jett Psaris and Marlena Lyons

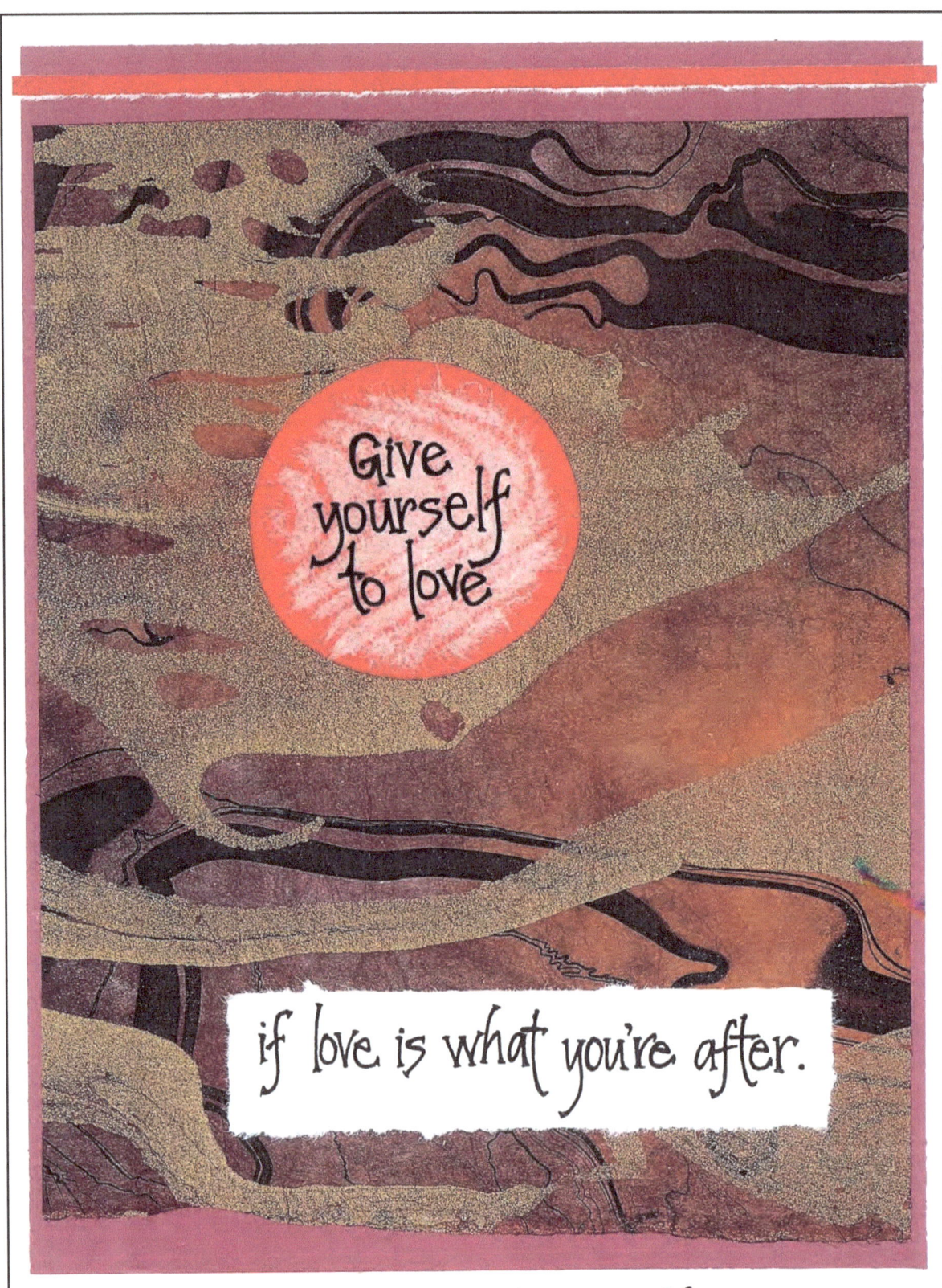

Give
yourself
to love

if love is what you're after.

Kate Wolf

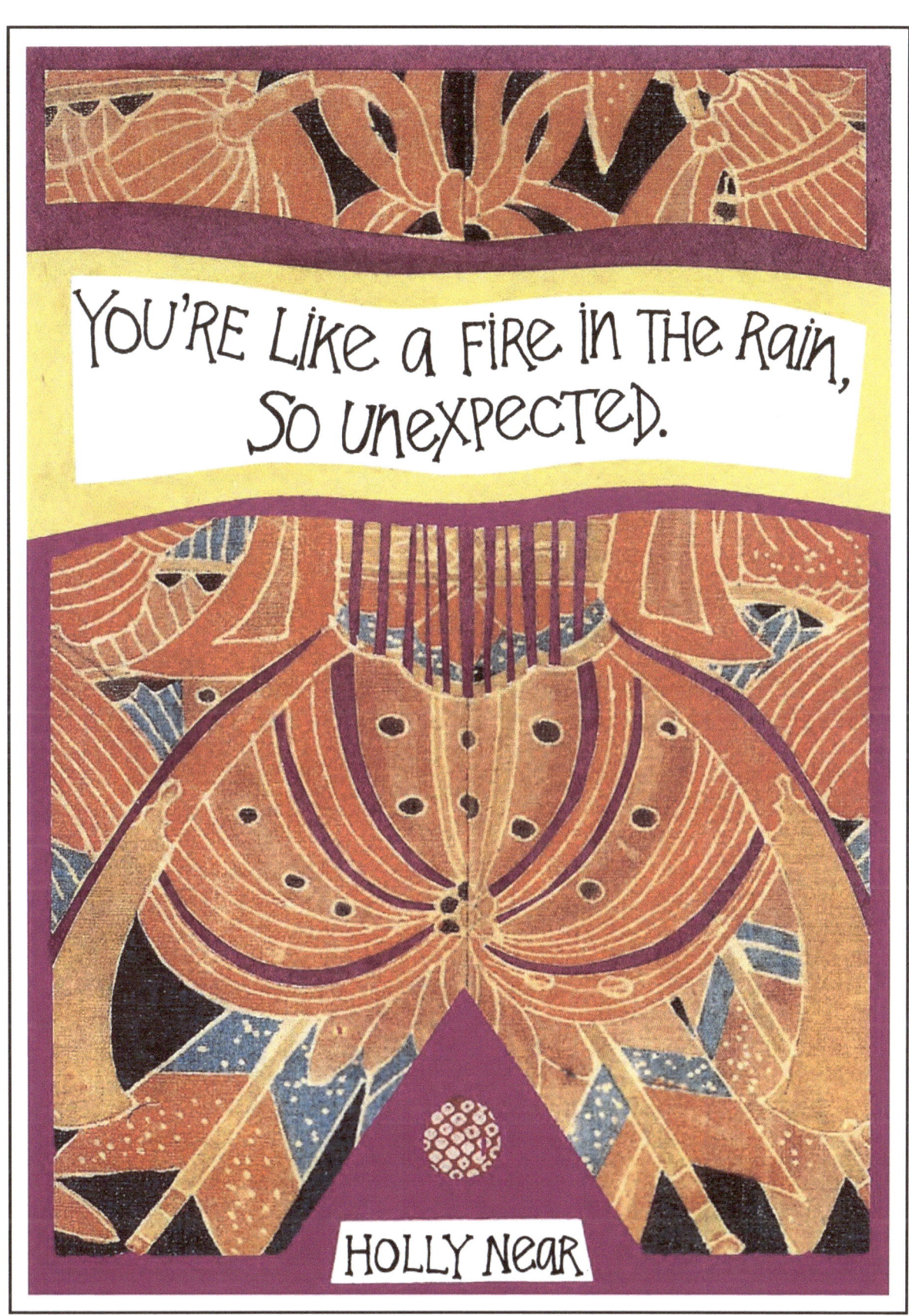

YOU'RE LIKE a FIRE IN THE RaIN, SO UNEXPECTED.

HOLLY NEaR

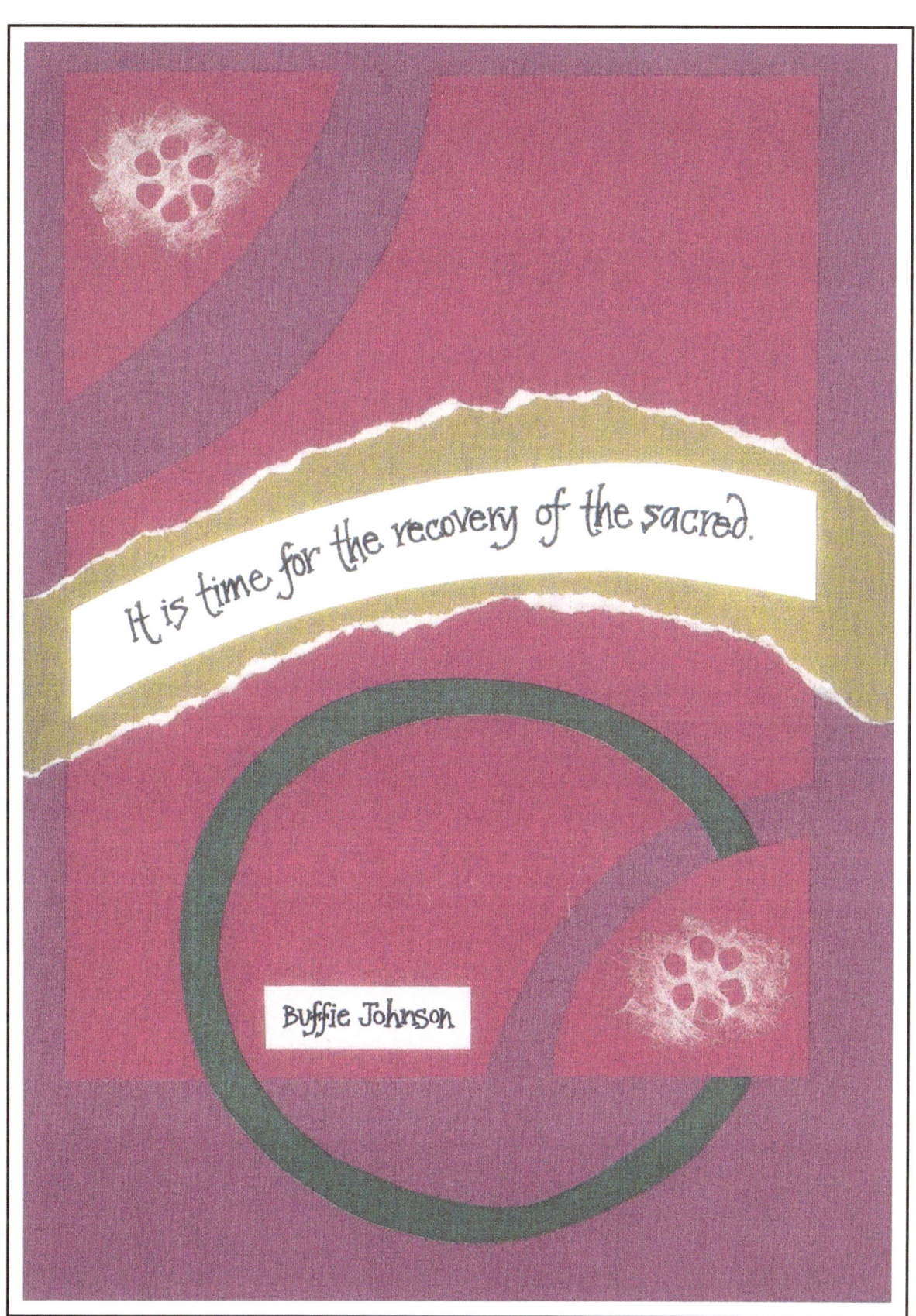

It is time for the recovery of the sacred.

Buffie Johnson

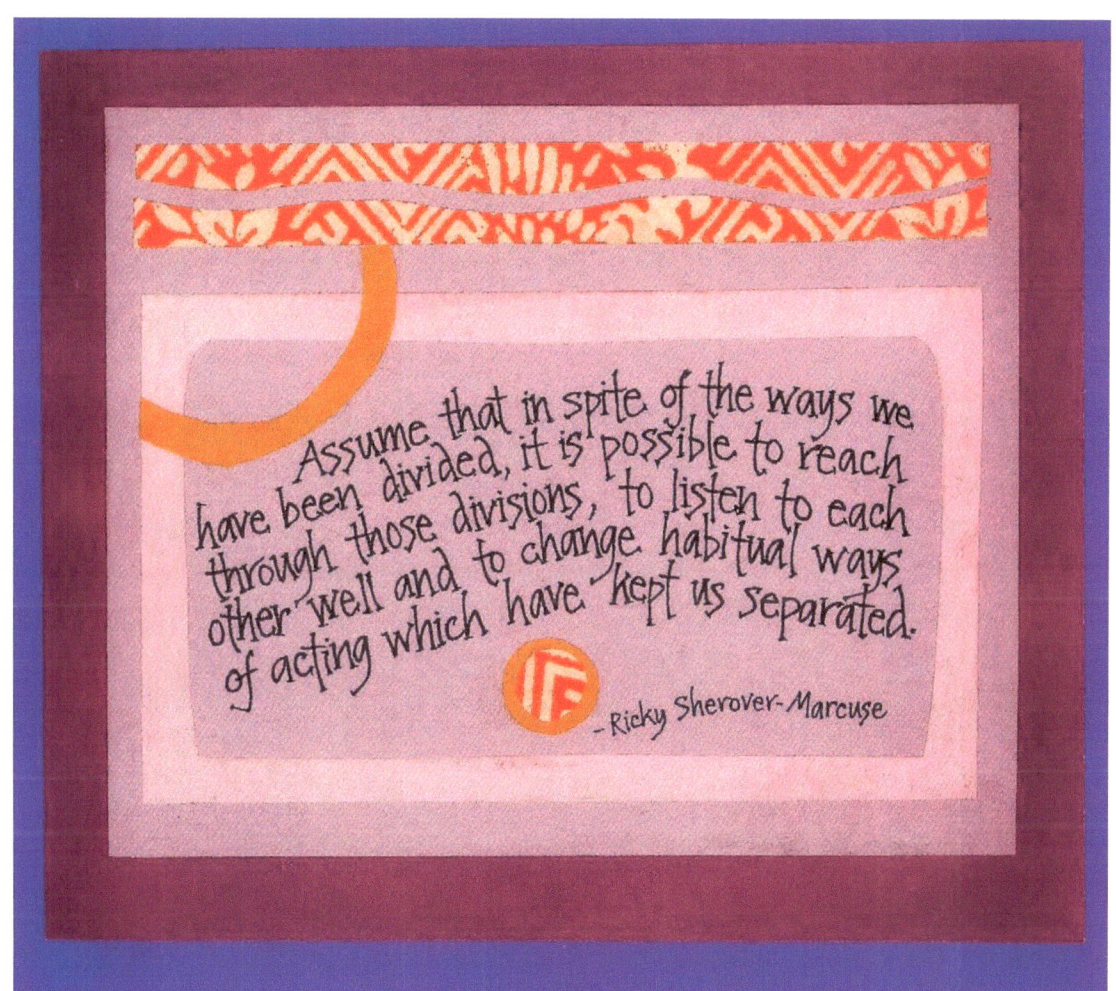

Assume that in spite of the ways we have been divided, it is possible to reach through those divisions, to listen to each other well and to change habitual ways of acting which have kept us separated.

— Ricky Sherover-Marcuse

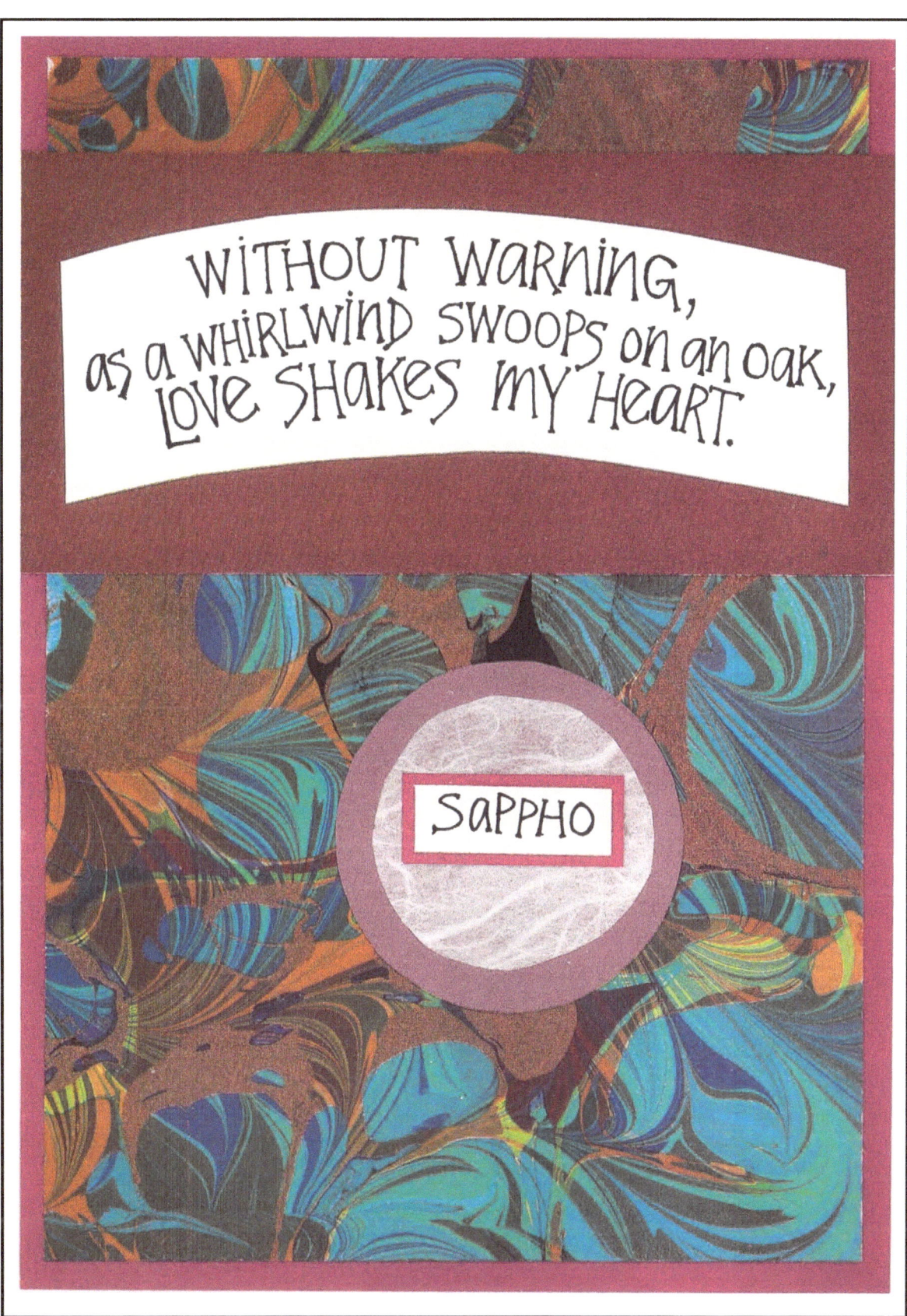

WITHOUT WARNING,
as a WHIRLWIND SWOOPS on an oak,
LOVE SHAKES MY HEART.

SAPPHO

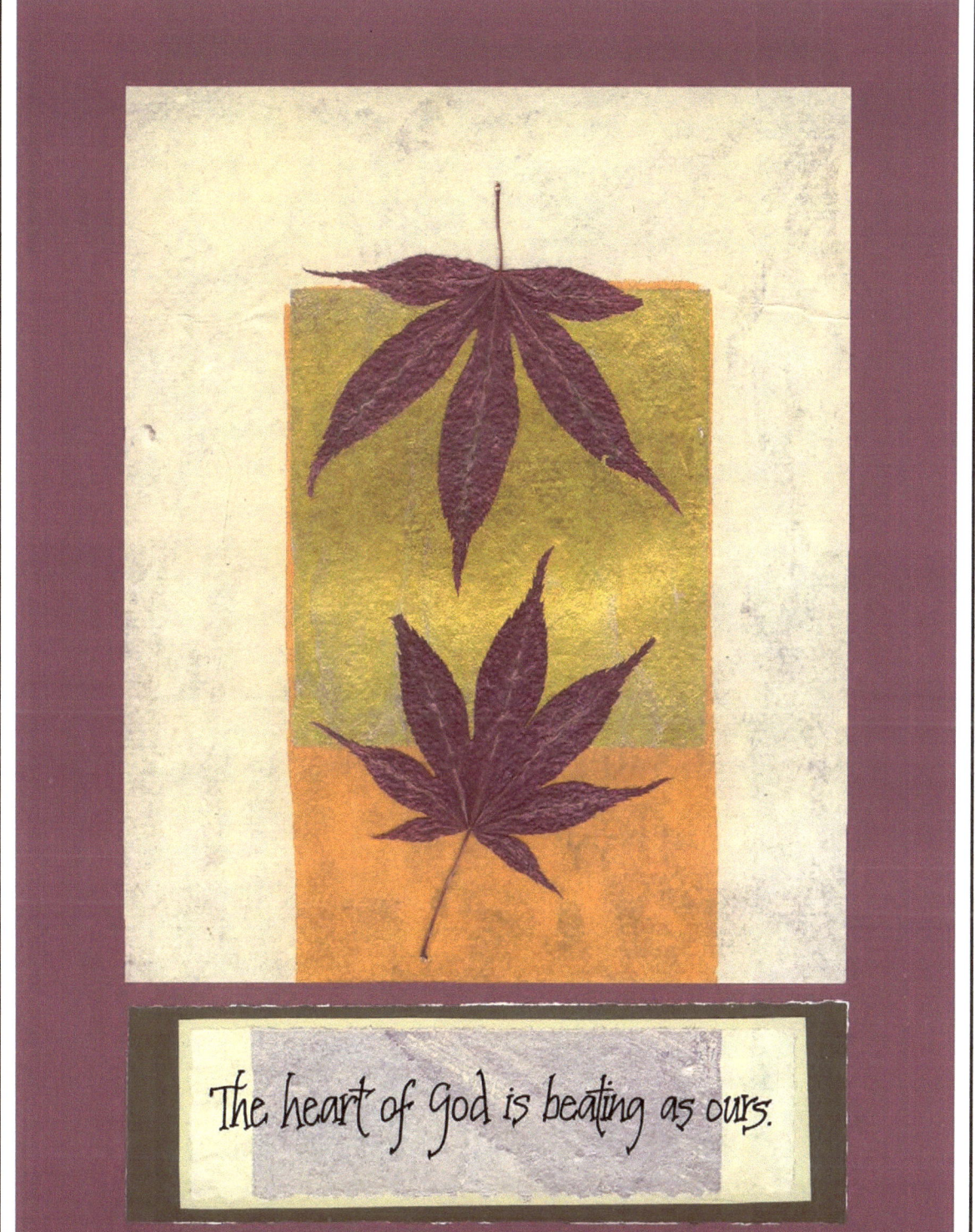

The heart of God is beating as ours.

Jennifer Bonadio

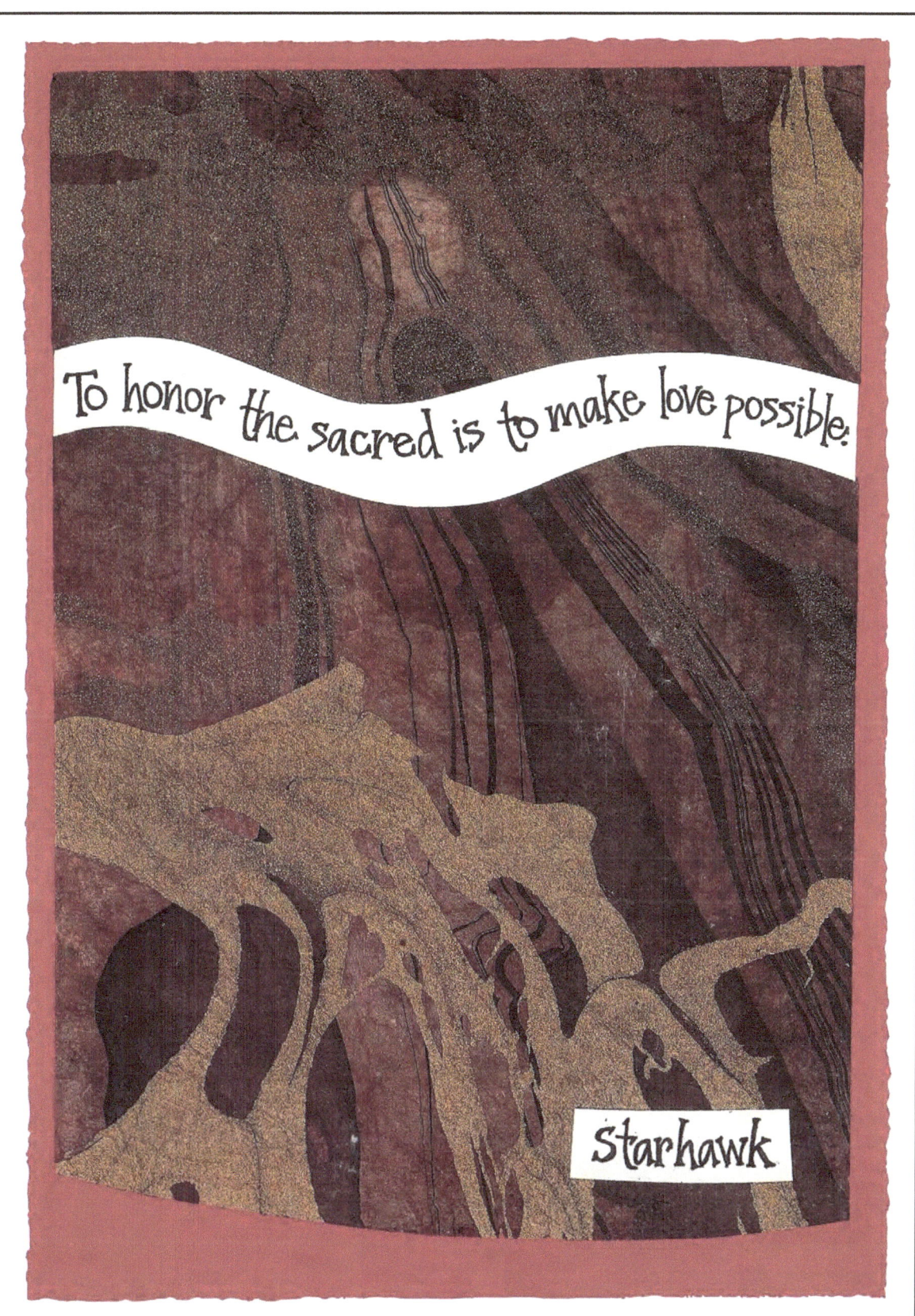

To honor the sacred is to make love possible.

Starhawk

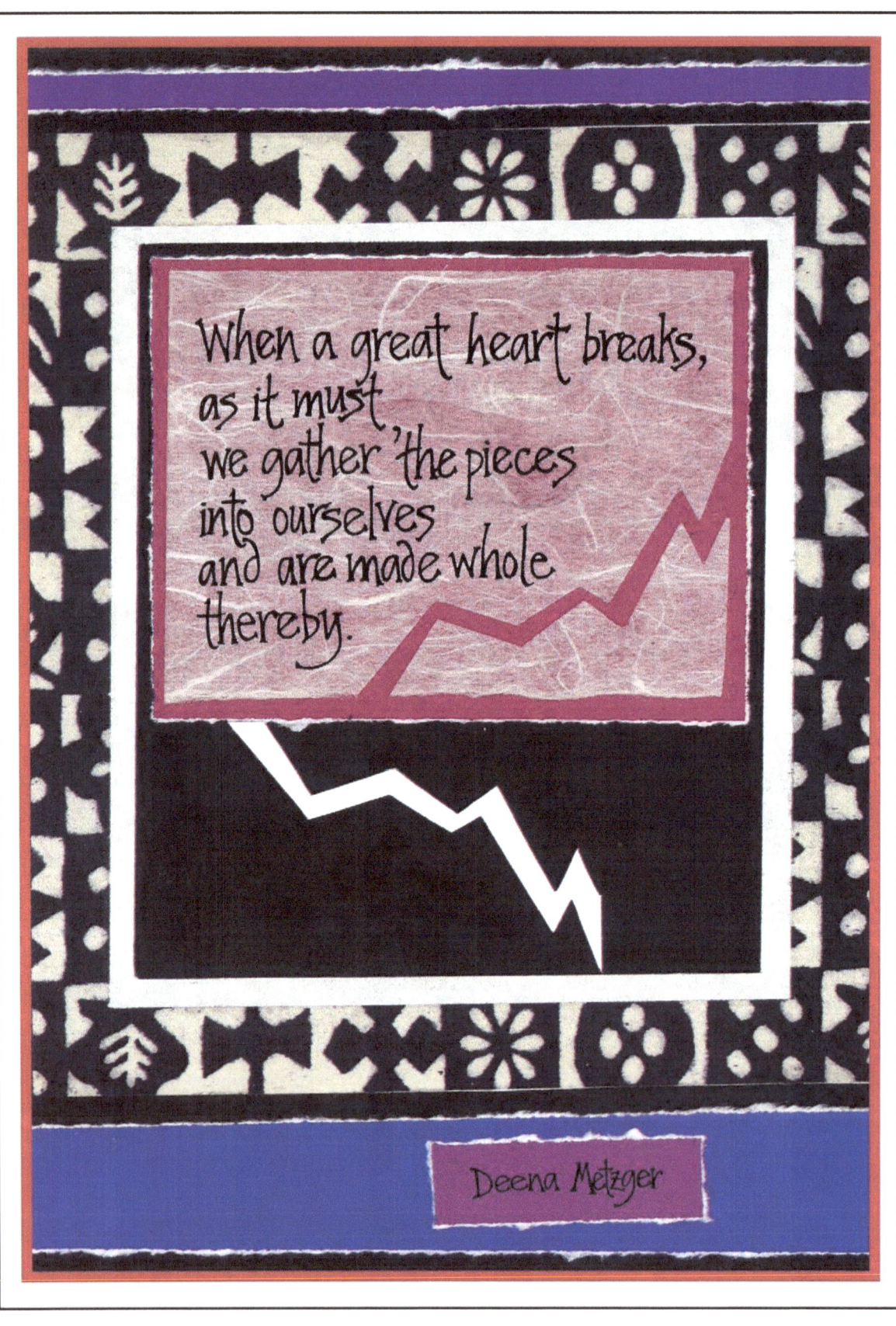

When a great heart breaks,
as it must
we gather the pieces
into ourselves
and are made whole
thereby.

Deena Metzger

THE new Face i TURN UP TO YOU
no one else on eaRTH Has ever seen.

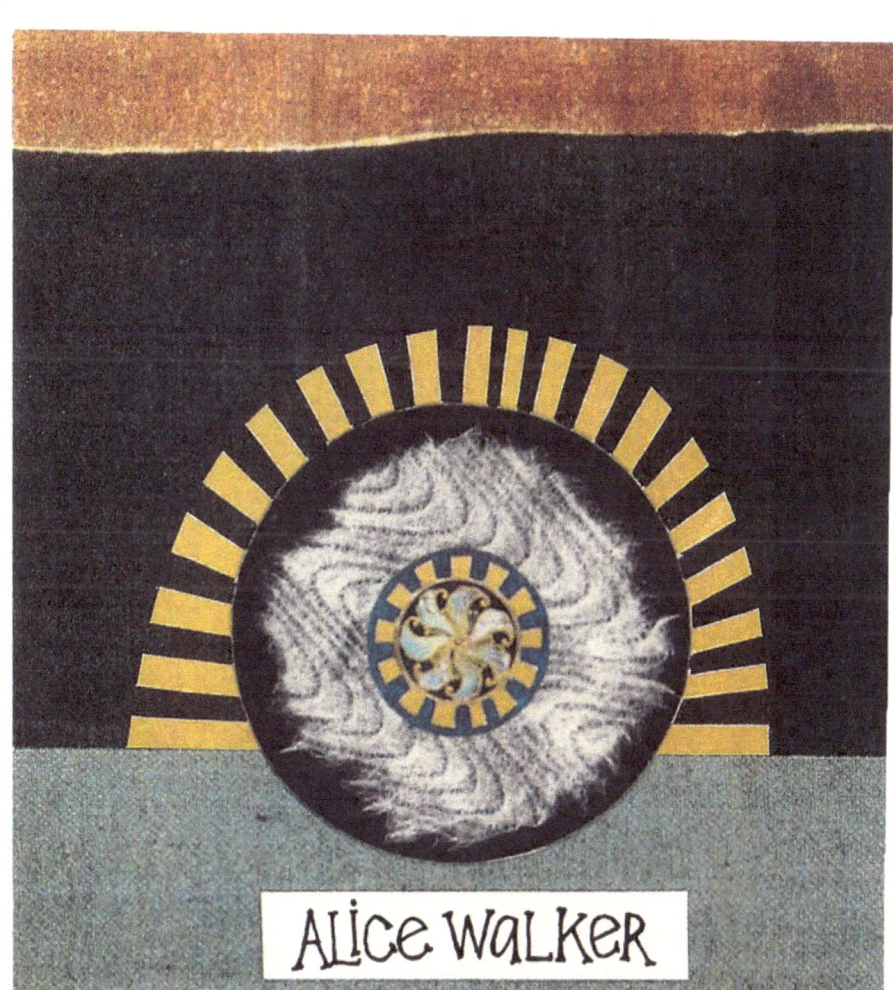

ALICE WALKER

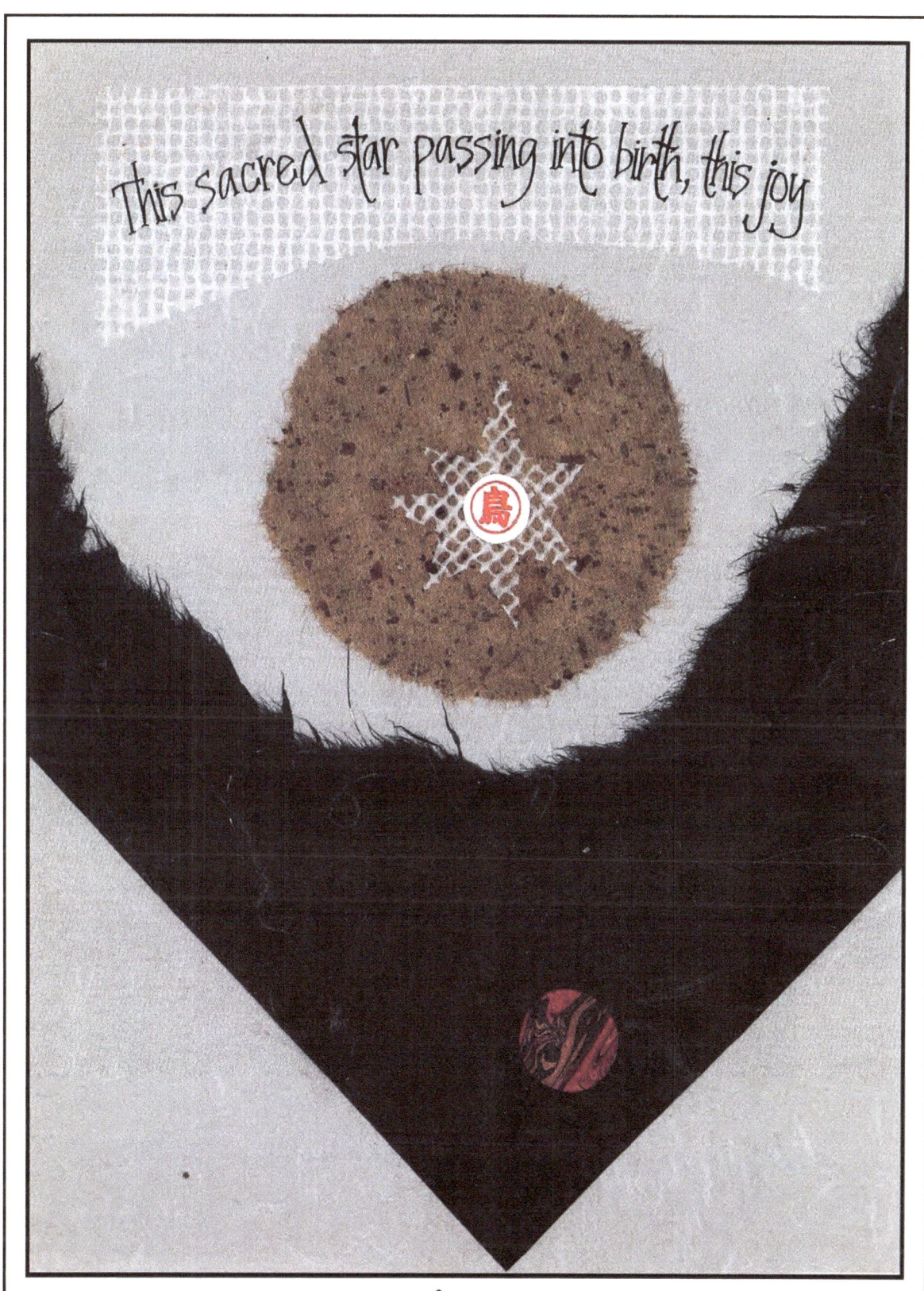

This sacred star passing into birth, this joy

Chellis Glendinning

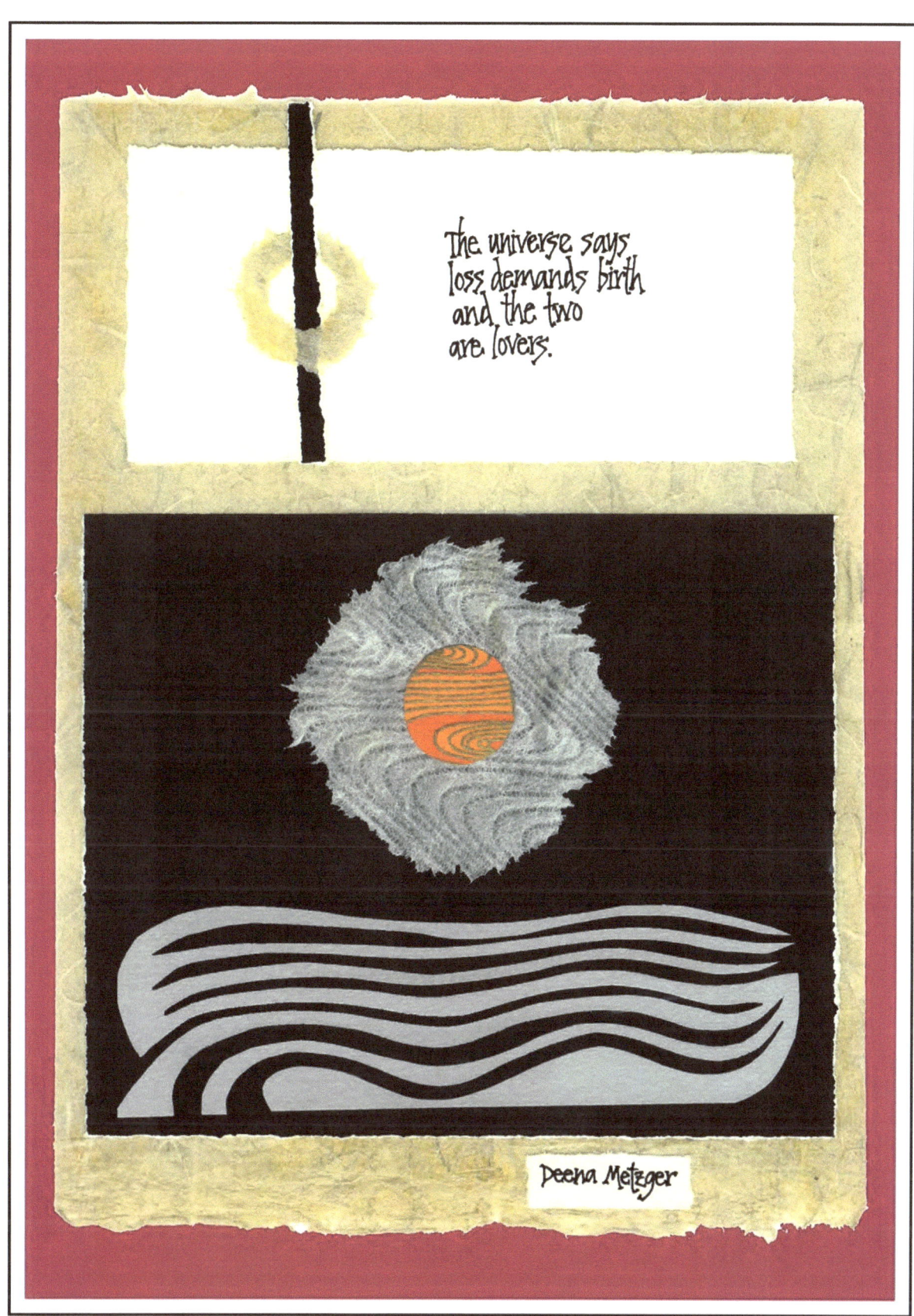

The universe says
loss demands birth
and the two
are lovers.

Deena Metzger

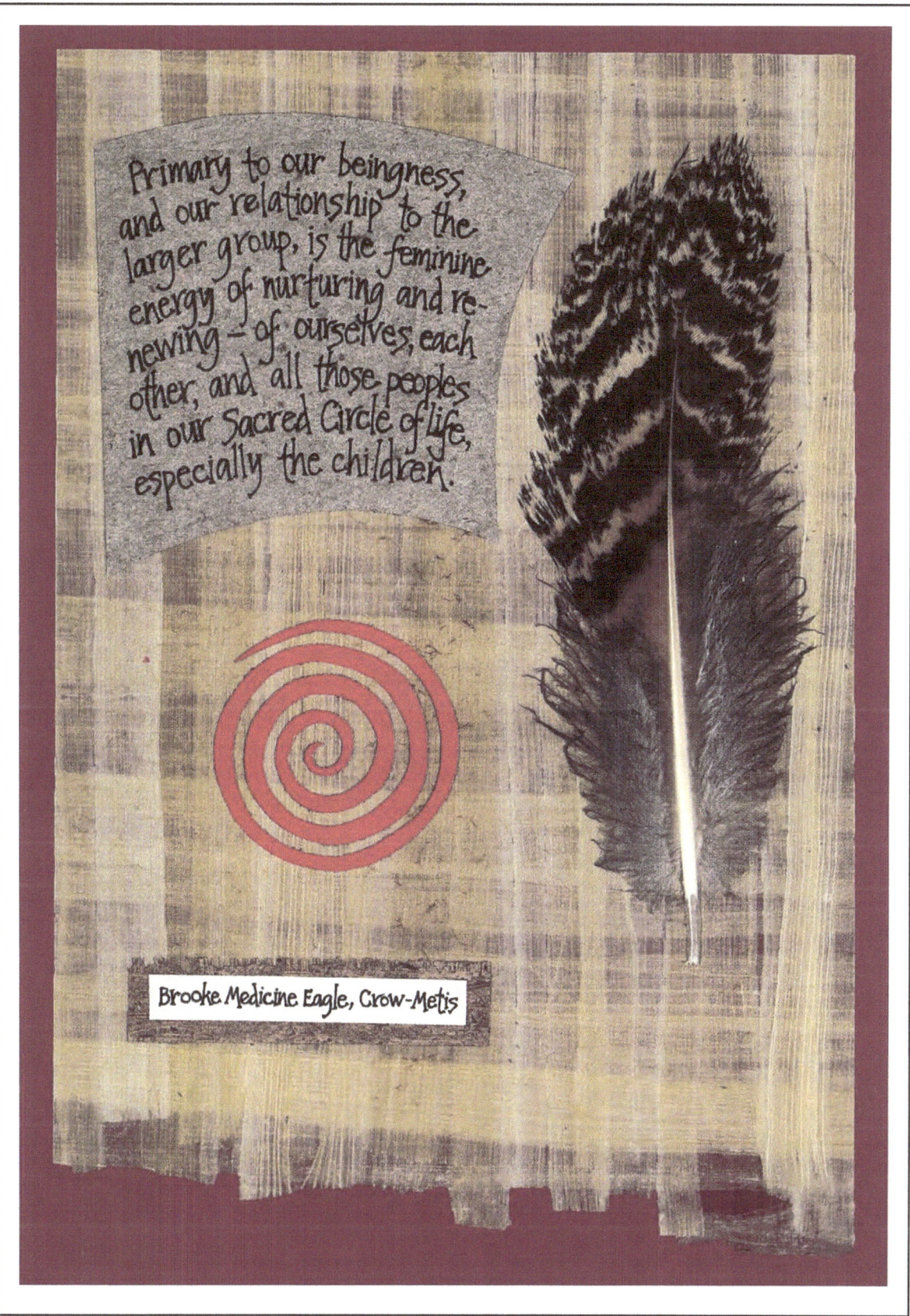

Primary to our beingness, and our relationship to the larger group, is the feminine energy of nurturing and re- newing — of ourselves, each other, and all those peoples in our Sacred Circle of life, especially the children.

Brooke Medicine Eagle, Crow-Metis

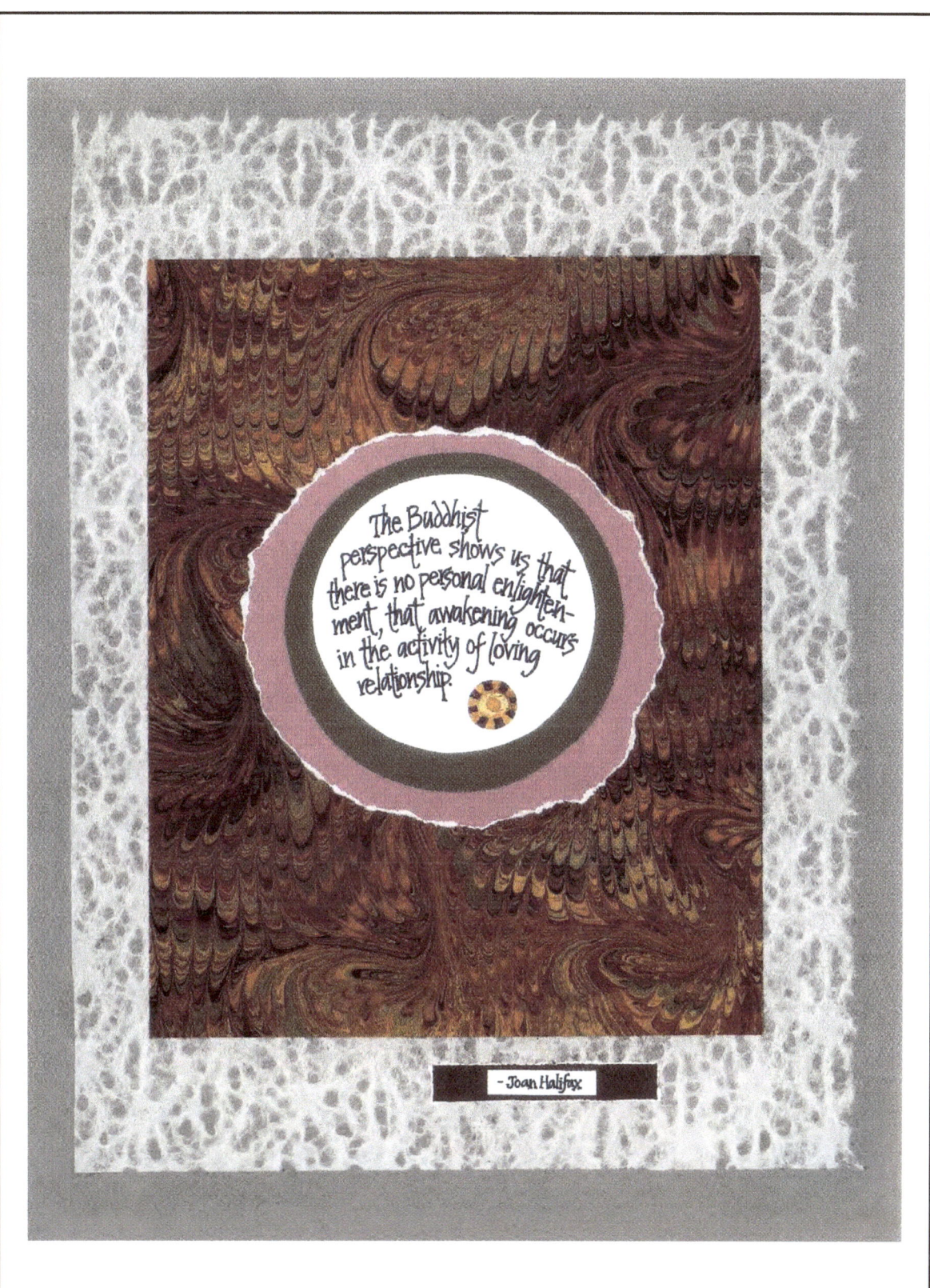

The Buddhist perspective shows us that there is no personal enlightenment, that awakening occurs in the activity of loving relationship.

– Joan Halifax

SMALL THINGS DONE IN GREAT LOVE
BRING JOY AND PEACE.

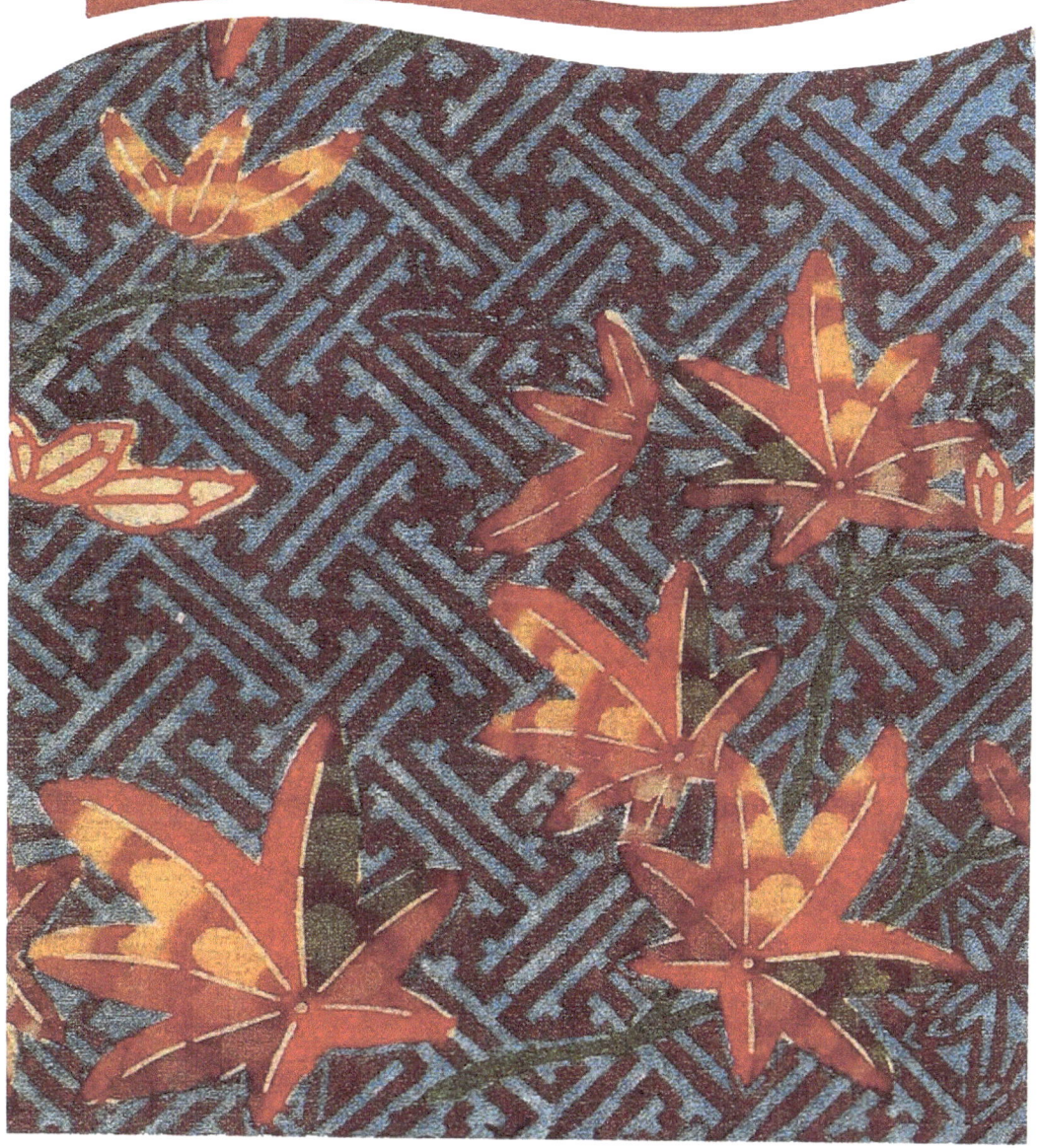

Mother Teresa

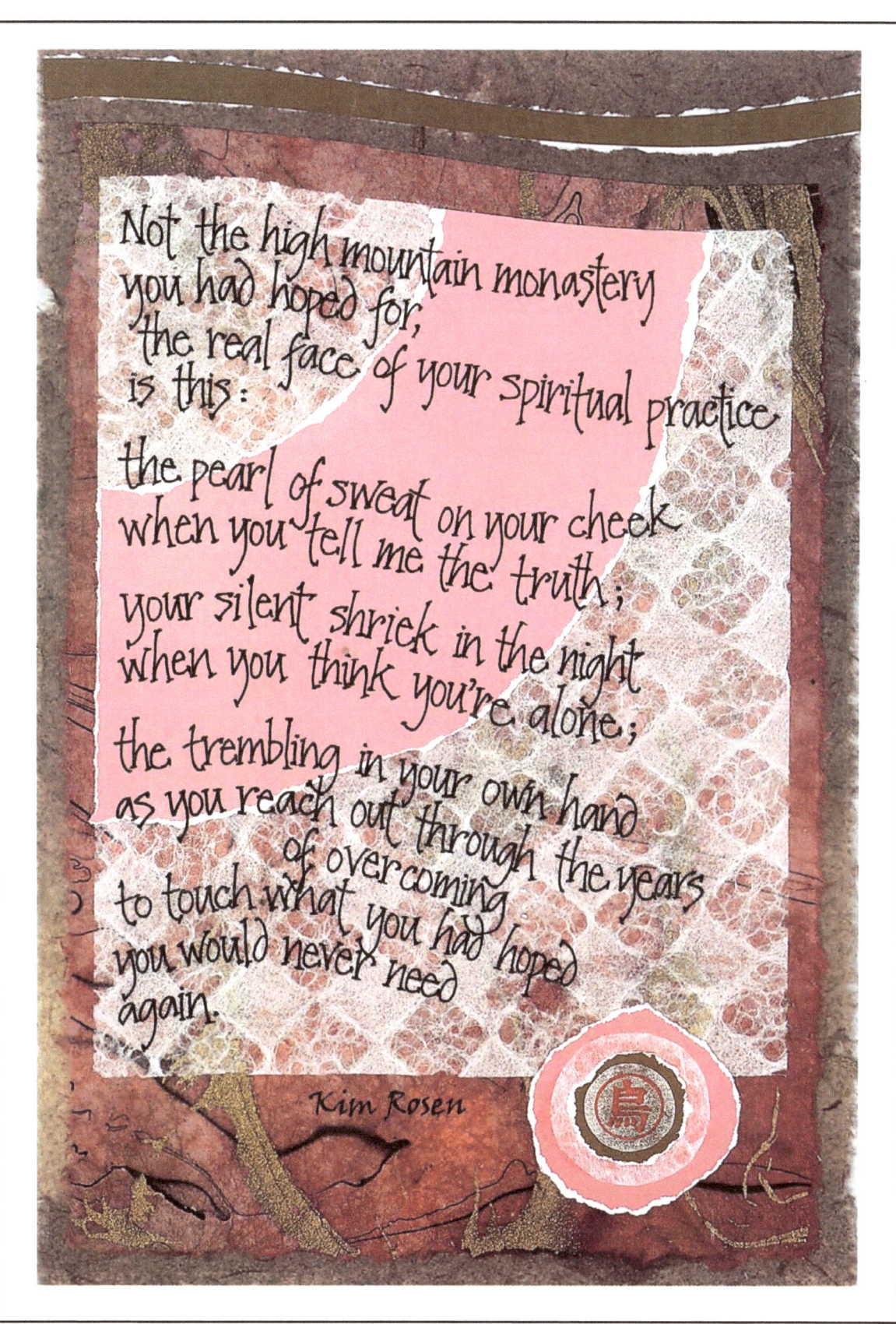

Not the high mountain monastery
you had hoped for,
the real face of your spiritual practice
is this:

the pearl of sweat on your cheek
when you tell me the truth;
your silent shriek in the night
when you think you're alone;

the trembling in your own hand
as you reach out through the years
of overcoming
to touch what you had hoped
you would never need
again.

Kim Rosen

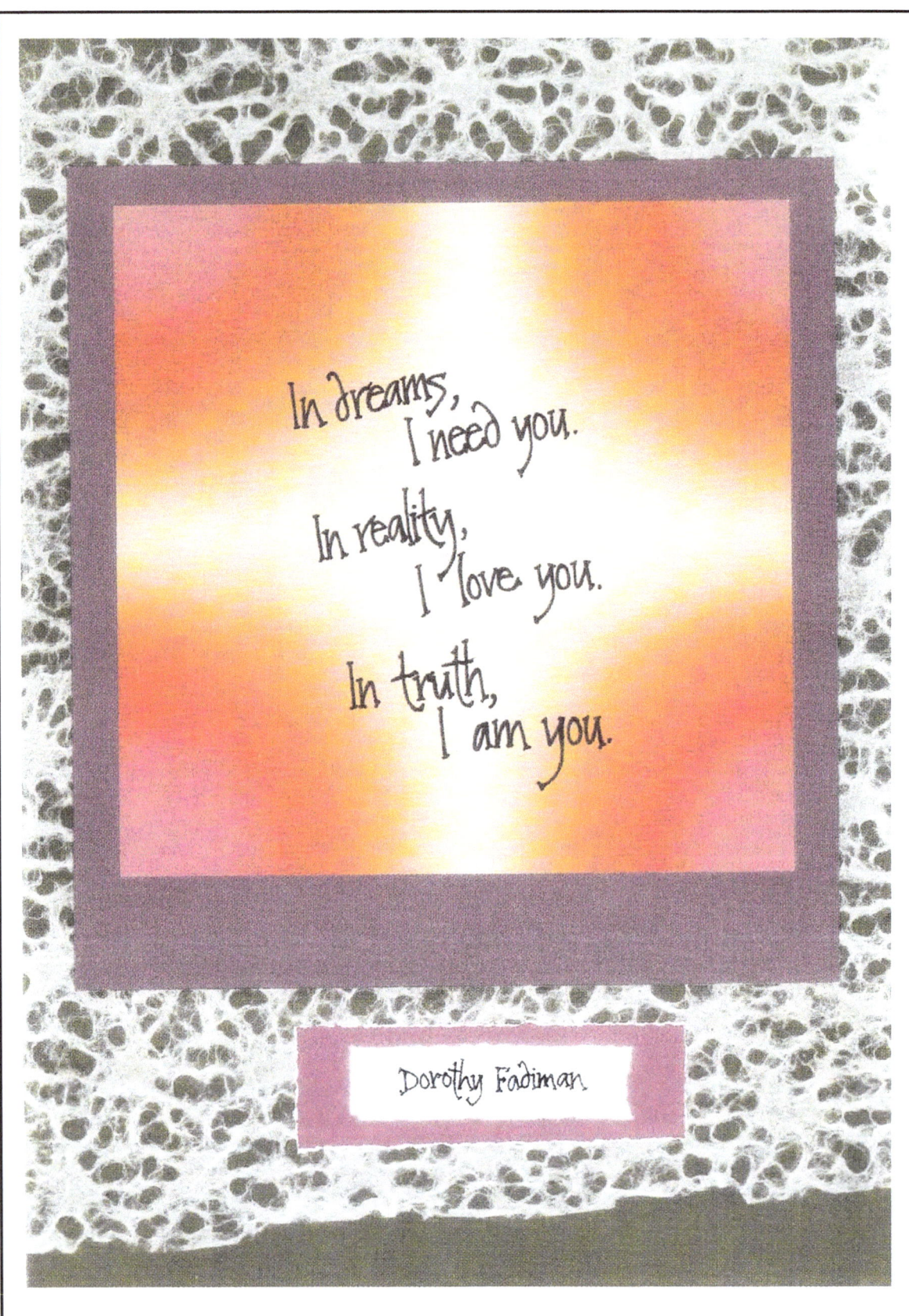

In dreams,
I need you.

In reality,
I love you.

In truth,
I am you.

Dorothy Fadiman

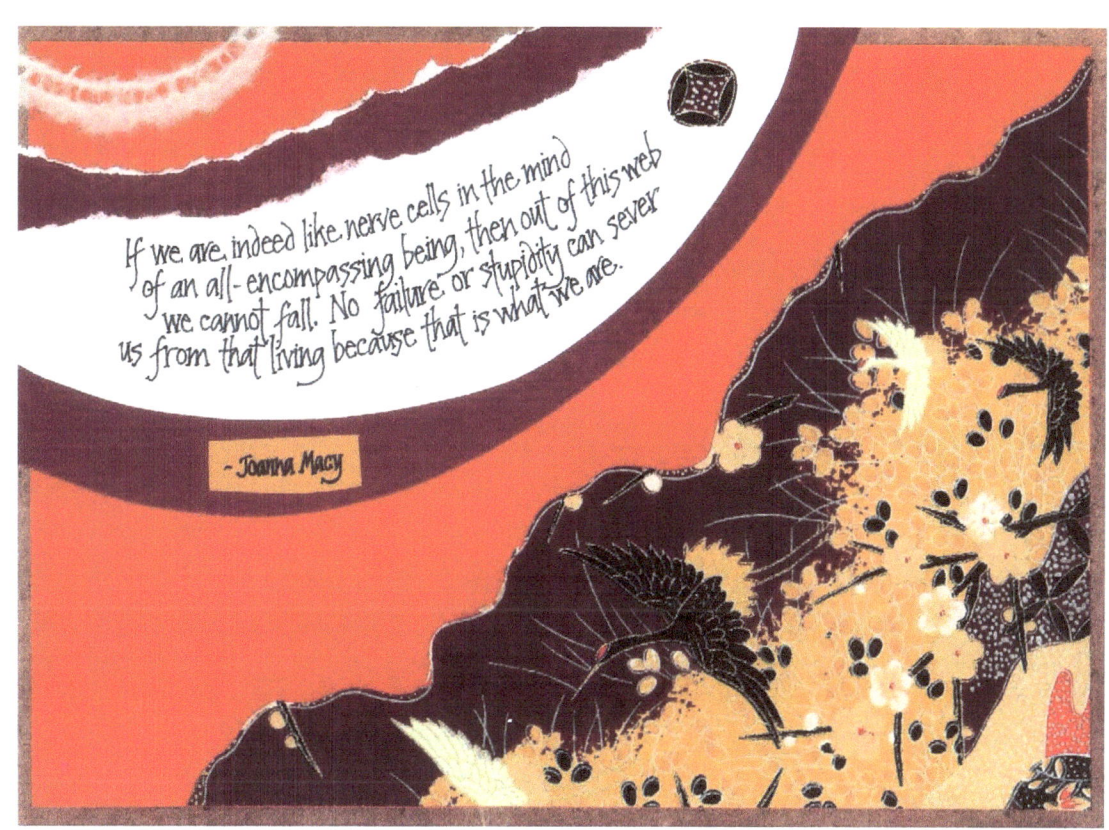

If we are, indeed like nerve cells in the mind of an all-encompassing being, then out of this web we cannot fall. No failure or stupidity can sever us from that living because that is what we are.

~ Joanna Macy

Drown me in your eyes.
Please! Drown me in your eyes!
Let them penetrate my fear
with their compassion
until all doubt has vanished.
Let their undertow destroy
this ignorance called Separation
until there is no shred of you or me.
Let them speak where words cannot,
pulling me into the silence
of Love's annihilation.

Drown me in your eyes.
Please! Drown me in your eyes!
Submerge me in their knowing
far beneath my concepts;
teach me to breathe in their waters.
Undress me in their Truth
until there's nothing to hide
and nakedness contains no skin or shame.
Swallow me in their seeing
until nothing is left except what's Real
and nothing is seen that is not.

Drown me in your eyes.
Please! Drown me in your eyes!
Immerse me in their clear Awareness
undisturbed by thoughts or dreams
or notions of being bound or freed.
Dissolve me in your eyes until no I exists
who imagines she sees God in them
but only God seeing God through God.
And when I gasp and thrash, begging to return
from Love's reflection of my Self,
hold me in your gaze until I die.

Dorothy Hunt

I WILL NOT DIE AN UNLIVED LIFE.
I WILL NOT LIVE IN FEAR
OF FALLING OR CATCHING FIRE.
I CHOOSE TO INHABIT MY DAYS,
TO ALLOW MY LIVING TO OPEN ME,
TO MAKE ME LESS AFRAID,
MORE ACCESSIBLE,
TO LOOSEN MY HEART
UNTIL IT BECOMES A WING,
A TORCH, A PROMISE.
I CHOOSE TO RISK MY SIGNIFICANCE;
TO LIVE
SO THAT WHICH CAME TO ME AS SEED
GOES TO THE NEXT AS BLOSSOM
AND THAT WHICH CAME
TO ME AS BLOSSOM,
GOES ON AS FRUIT.

Dawna Markova

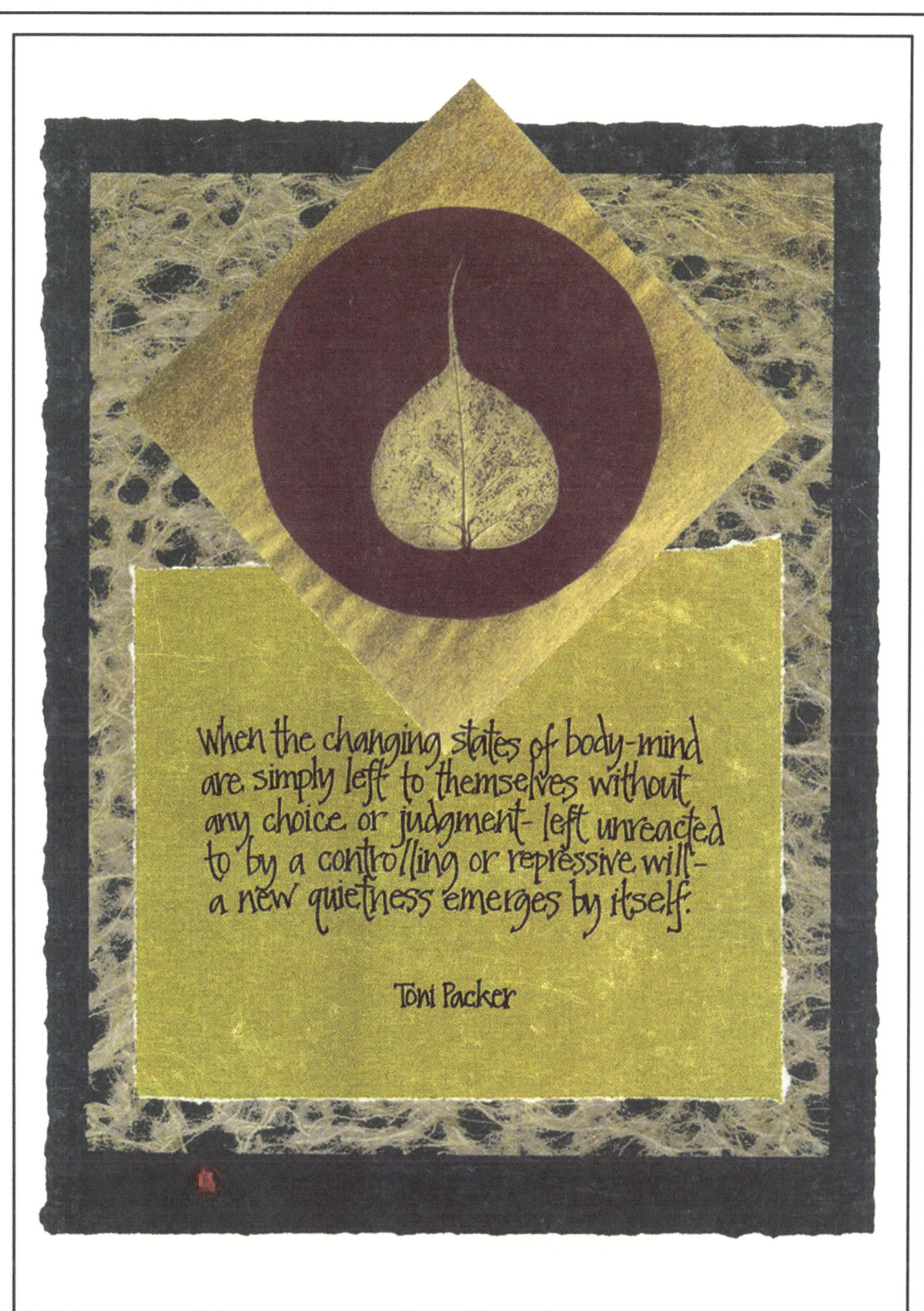

When the changing states of body-mind
are simply left to themselves without
any choice or judgment- left unreacted
to by a controlling or repressive will-
a new quietness emerges by itself.

Toni Packer

Your Self is already inherently liberated. It is the ideas that have been imposed on that Self which must be set free.

Gangaji

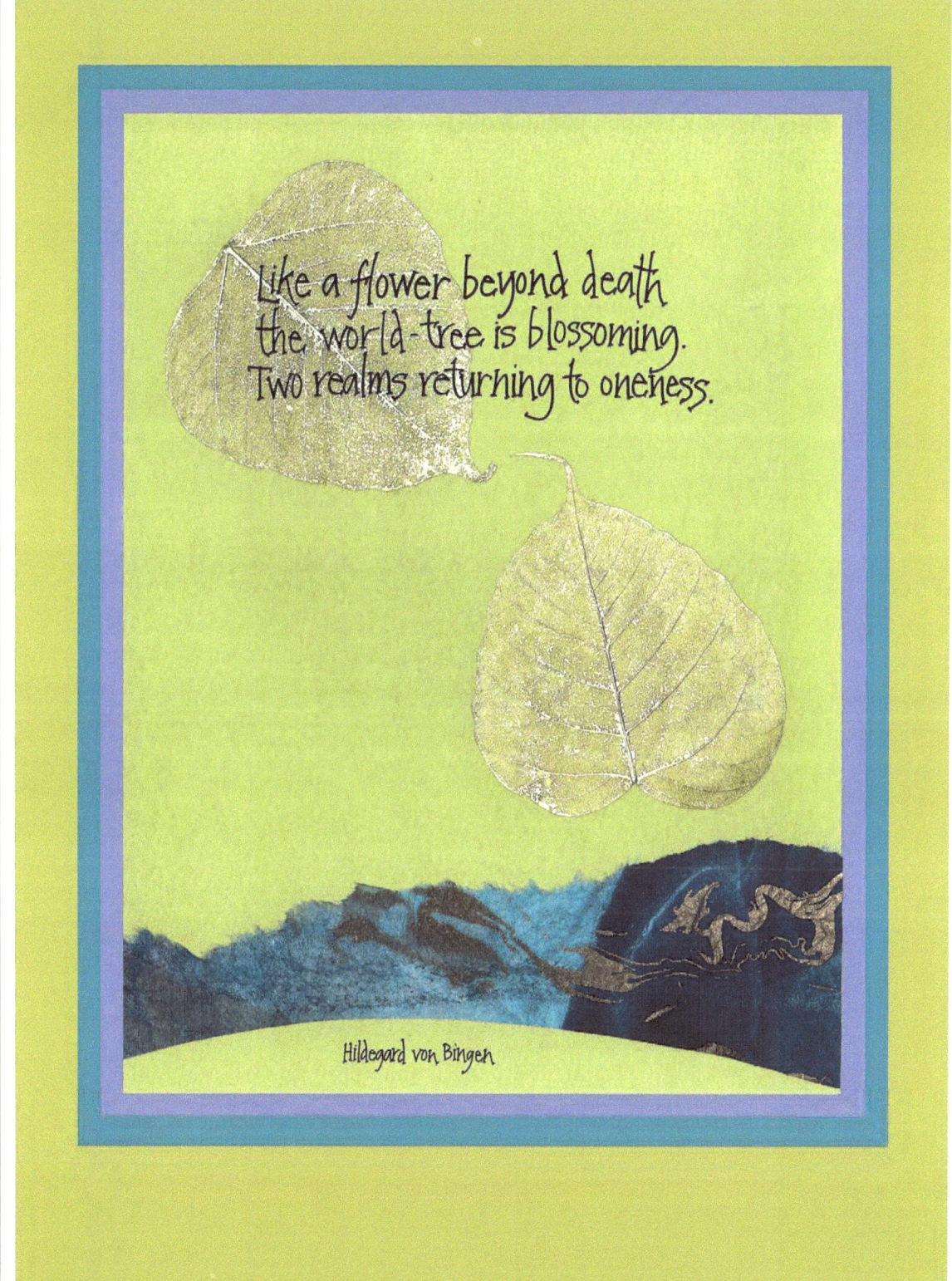

Like a flower beyond death
the world-tree is blossoming.
Two realms returning to oneness.

Hildegard von Bingen

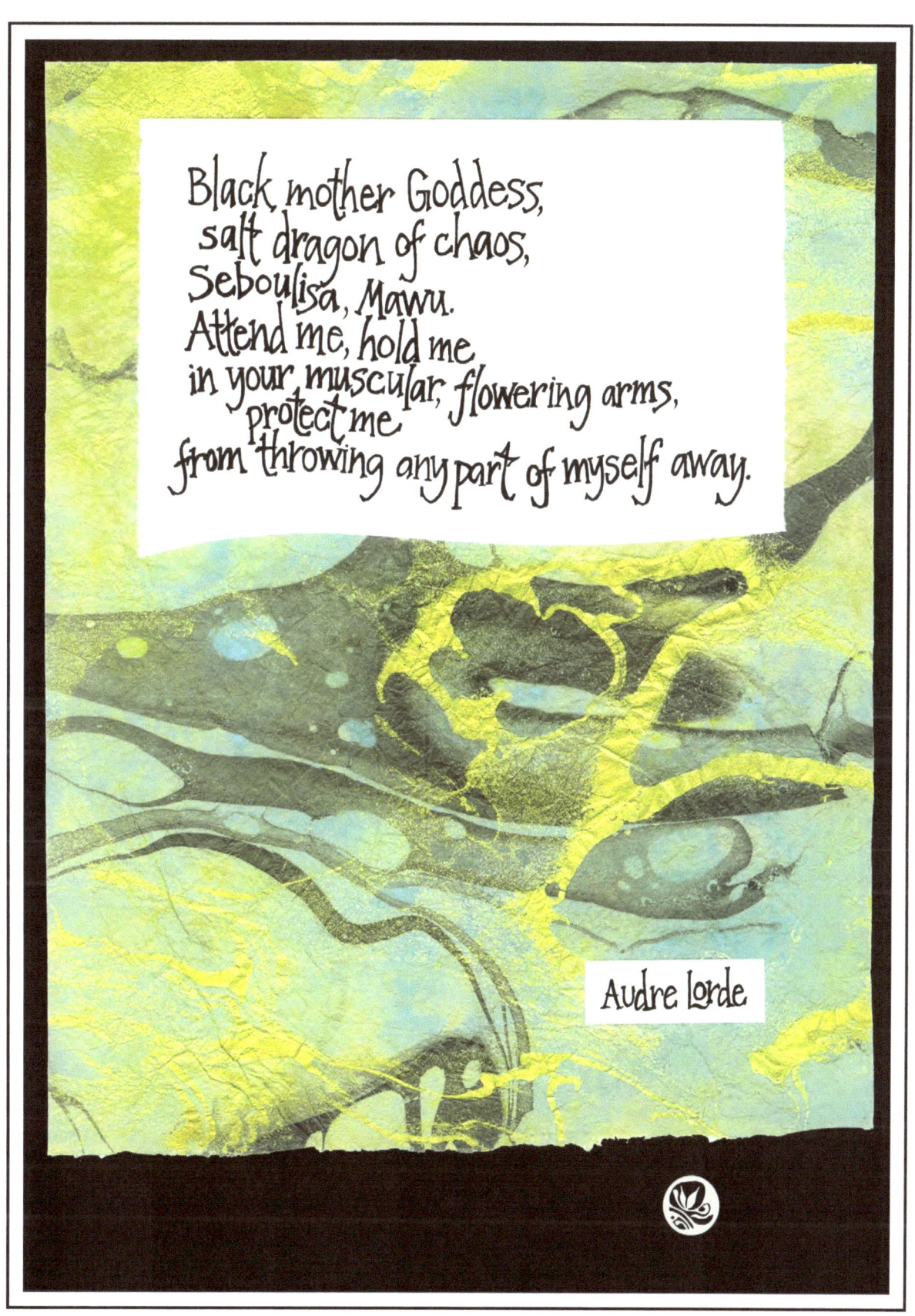

Black mother Goddess,
salt dragon of chaos,
Seboulisa, Mawu.
Attend me, hold me
in your muscular, flowering arms,
protect me
from throwing any part of myself away.

Audre Lorde

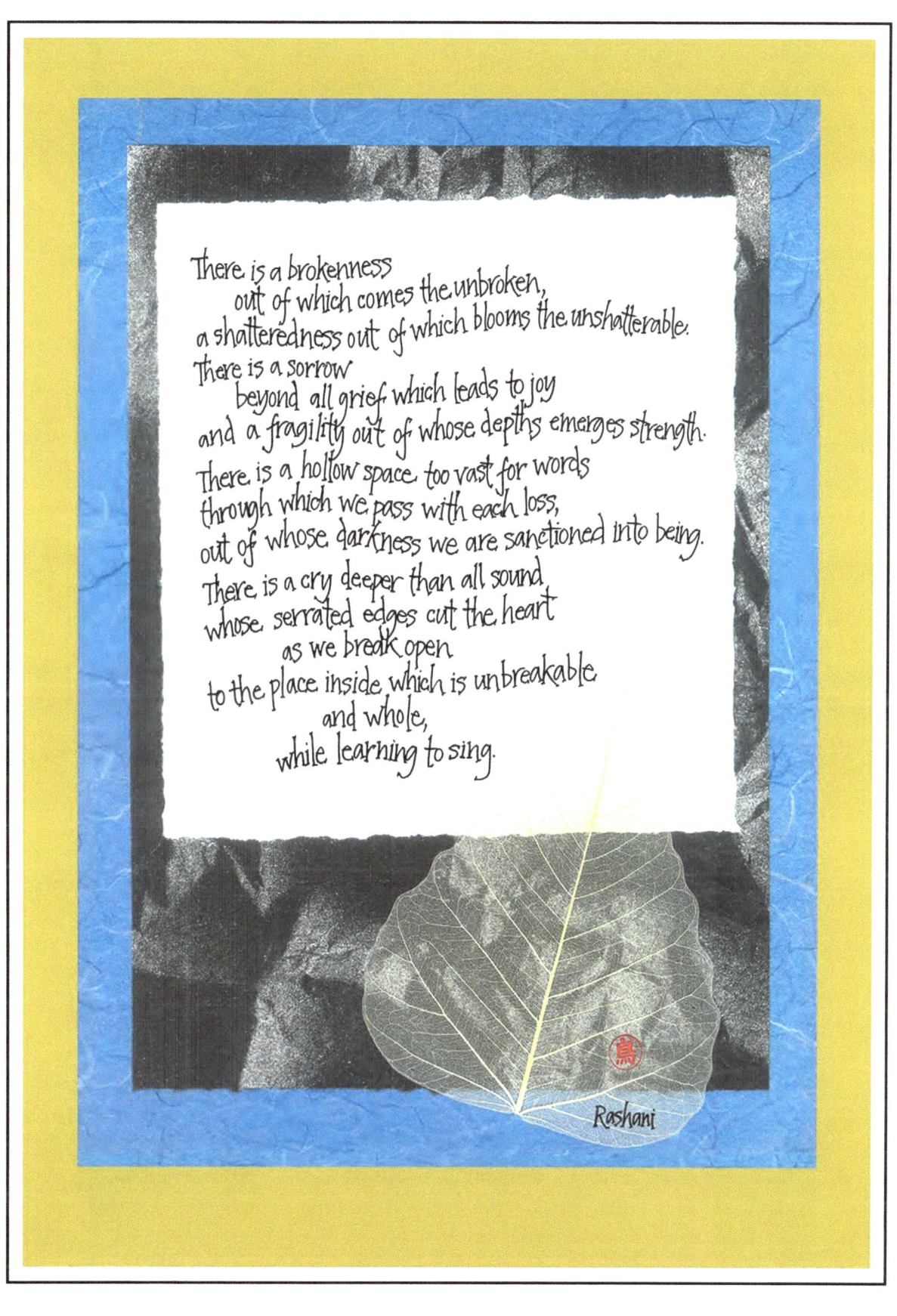

There is a brokenness
      out of which comes the unbroken,
a shatteredness out of which blooms the unshatterable.
There is a sorrow
      beyond all grief which leads to joy
and a fragility out of whose depths emerges strength.
There is a hollow space too vast for words
through which we pass with each loss,
out of whose darkness we are sanctioned into being.
There is a cry deeper than all sound
whose serrated edges cut the heart
      as we break open
to the place inside which is unbreakable
      and whole,
      while learning to sing.

Rashani

Afterwords

I in no way intend to show favoritism to the women whose words are present in my collages, as opposed to other women whose words are not included. My collages simply represent a very small percentage of the many women whose lives interwove with—and became part of—mine, and whose presence made a difference in my evolutionary unfolding. The "Woman's Collection" of greeting cards includes 116 collages, which you can see on my website:

http://rashani.com/dharma-gaia-cards/Relationships/Womens.html

Instead of putting the collages in chronological order I arranged them according to their colors, which offers more of a visual flow. For those interested in the dates that they were designed, here is a list, as they appear in the book:

1) Joan Larkin: 1988
2) Rashani Réa: 1988
3) Tsultrim Allione: 1990
4) Anonymous: 1990
5) Chellis Glindenning: 1990
6) Geneen Roth: 1991
7) Gangaji: 2000
8) Peace Pilgrim: 1993
9) Alice Walker: 1992
10) Christina Harris: 1993
11) Doreen Valiente: 1991
12) Helen Keller: 1991
13) Rabia: 1994
14) Sonia Johnson: 1991
15) Women's Environment
    and Development Organization: 1992
16) Toni Packer: 1991
17) Sedonia Cahill: 1992
18) Anaïs Nin: 1990
19) Lalla: 2001
20) Kirtana: 2000
21) Pema Chödrön: 2001
22) Jeanette Delmar: 2001
23) Ricky Sherover-Marcuse: 1990
24) Emilie Conrad: 2001
25) Starhawk: 1989
26) Dianthus: 1990
27: Dhyani Ywahoo: 1991
28) Buffie Johnson: 1991
29) Juju of Ka`u: 2005
30) Holly Near: 1990
31) Elisabeth Kübler-Ross: 1992
32) Audre Lorde: 1991

33) Etty Hillesum: 1991
34) Susan Griffin: 1993
35) Kathleen Raine: 1991
36) Dhyani Ywahoo: 1991
37) Ann Herbert: 1991
38) Jett Psaris and Marlena Lyons: 2000
39) Dominie Cappadonna: 1991
40) Clarissa Pinkola Estés: 1990
41) Ma Anandamayi: 2000
42) Jett Psaris and Marlena Lyons: 2000
43) Kate Wolf: 1992
44) Holly Near: 1989
45) Buffie Johnson: 1991
46) Ricky Sherover-Marcuse: 1990
47) Sappho: 1989
48) Jennifer Bonadio: 2005
49) Starhawk: 1989
50) Deena Metzger: 1991
51) Alice Walker: 1993
52) Chellis Glindenning: 1993
53) Deena Metzger: 1991
54) Brooke Medicine Eagle: 1991
55) Joan Halifax: 1991
56) Mother Teresa: 1990
57) Kim Rosen: 2000
58) Dorothy Fadiman: 1989
59) Joanna Macy: 1991
60) Dorothy Hunt: 2005
61) Dawna Markova: 1991
62) Toni Packer: 1998
63) Gangaji: 2000
64) Hildegard von Bingen: 1995
65) Audre Lorde: 1995
66) Rashani Réa: 1991